STORIES TO TELL

Unlocking the Creative Mind

Jack Heslop
Amy Kitching
T. Kitching
Tapiwa MacHin
C.R. Mallett
K. Ngai
Joe Ryan

Edited by Anita Belli

ISBN: 10: 154804569
ISBN-13: 978 – 1548048563

BOOKS
www.hardpressedbooks.co.uk

Front Cover Image; K. Ngai
Back Cover Image: C.R. Mallett
Cover Design: Charlie Peacock

DEDICATION

*To the Writers
and Artists
of Tomorrow*

Contents

ACKNOWLEDGMENTS

We would like to thank our programme coordinator, Georgeta Busuioc, Talent Match Specialist Mentor, for making it happen, and all her colleagues from Talent Match South East -Essex hub, for supporting the funding of this Creative Writing Course. The Mayor, Pam Morrison 2016-17, and Councilor Garry Calver; the staff of the Guildhall Harwich; Lucy Ballard, Michelle Townsend, Peter Barrenger and Briony Burrows, for enabling us to use the Guildhall, which inspired us with its beauty and history. To Chris and John Theobald and the Harwich Society volunteers of The Redoubt, Harwich, for a thought provoking day of stories and inspiration. Also to John Theobald for offering his skills as a professional photographer. To Mary and David Oxley, of Oxleys, Dovercourt, for feeding the body and the creative mind. To Charlie Peacock for turning our visual ideas into a cover design, and to Gerald Hornsby's eagle eye in searching out the gremlins in our text. Special thanks also to author and writing tutor Anita Belli for taking us on a creative journey into our own stories. Finally, to fellow participants who made the course what it was, a huge thank you for supporting each other with a spirit of generosity and openness.

FOREWORD

By Jack Heslop

Throughout the course that inspired this book we, the writers, collected material at an almost frightening pace, surprised perhaps by our own abilities to create. Such is the way with creativity. Everyone has an ability, but confidence enough to make that first step, to sit down and actually write, or draw, or whatever, can be hard to come by.

This book contains a selection of stories, poems, drawings, and extracts from writing exercises undertaken throughout our sessions. The genres of these works include children's fiction, science fiction a ghost story, manga (the

Japanese comic-book art style,) a sonnet and free verse. (It's an... *eclectic* collection: Stephen King meets J.K. Rowling meets *Star Trek*, with a bit of Pam Ayres thrown in for good measure.

If our group's time on the course has taught us (or, at least, me, and trust me, it's tough to teach me squat...) anything, it's that different writers have wildly different voices and ideas, different stories to tell, and when you gather a group of writers in a room what they produce can't necessarily be predicted.

The extracts from writing exercises have been included to illustrate the creative process, to show how creative writing comes about, just as a draughtsman's sketch becomes a painting. The exercises can even be tried at home (trust me, it's safe, unless you're trying to write on a speeding motorcycle, I guess...).

I hope you enjoy what follows, and that it inspires you too.

From a post on the writers' blog:
http://unboundstories.blogspot.co.uk/2017/05/developing-our-ideas-and-preparing-book.html
.

INTRODUCTION

By Anita Belli

It starts with ice, and a disparate group, and a need to thaw the rime of frost; to get to the deeper water where the stories lie, lurking beneath the surface of collective doubts, fears, anxieties, expectations, and just a frisson of excitement which warms the wood paneled room.

The Guildhall, Harwich: The Mayor in chains of office with Councillor Calver, welcome us to this historic place; a building full of stories which whisper from the walls and tease us with the graffiti of Napoleonic prisoners etched into the wood of the former cells.

Warm up, in a circle, on our feet; no hiding behind a desk; we are facing each other and like

3

a dancer, an athlete or musician, this will form the start of every session, preparing the mind and developing a collective focus on the stories we have to tell. Asking questions, being curious, playing games, digging deeper.

So why do we need to write a book?
Because stories are everywhere we look; in the lanes and on the beaches, the buildings and streets.

Stories are everywhere we go, from high street to hedgerow, from friend's flats to snapchat, we want everyone to know about the tit-for-tat; the dancing wombat; the cute cat...

We need to tell our friends and family what has happened to us; about the curious thing we saw from the window of the bus, or in the lane, or from the train. What's trending on twitter? Is it about us, or someone we know? Do we care? Why do we share?

Because it is a *story,* and stories matter, and life is one big story. Stories are happening all around us, every day, making up the rich tapestry of our lives.

This is *our* story. It is about our unique contribution to the world. We share, and care enough to tell it to others, whether it is a lesson learned, or points earned, some knowledge gained or the pain of love scorned or gifts pawned. Of love and loss, of family and friends. Whether it is the highs or lows, or the in between daze of our lives. The dull days, the cold and bleak and grey days; or the heat haze which brings us joy and refreshes our hopes and dreams. All united by the same human need; to tell it to the world in words or pictures; to mine our past and our imagination for stories and to harvest them. To look around and observe our here and now, looking for the funny, odd, unusual, moving, absurd stuff of life. To tell. To share. To learn. To care.

To bear witness to the here and now.

Our stories, living breathing things, flying high beside the stories of others.

Out There.

Let the games begin.

WARM UPS

In the beginning was a word... followed by another... taking each letter of the alphabet in turn....

Actually, Boris Couldn't Do Enough For Greta, However It Juxtaposed Knowingly, Loudly. Most Nuns Operate Privately, Quietly Reading Scriptures. Tomorrow, Unusually, Vows Will Xenophobically Yearn Zealously!

We abandoned the constraints of consecutive alphabet writing and made a random sentence, each following on from the previous speaker....

On a bright sunny day... a meteorite came crashing down ... followed swiftly by the bombs! As if that wasn't bad enough, Alice caught her husband with the houseboy!.... But what Boris didn't know was that his wife, Alice was also having an affair..... However, the bombs and the meteorite interrupted them somewhat!..... Then there was Donald Trump bombing Syria .... which made their situation seem less important .... so they all shacked up together..... in a shelter...!

And another day....

It was gory hell....You couldn't see the face; only the eyes popping out... It was everywhere; all over the windows....The house was old and hadn't been lived in for a very long time....The floorboards were broken and the windows shattered...And there he lay, in the middle of the room, slaughtered....No one quite knew what had happened to him.

This format was fun and we used it to draw out the key ingredients of 'story'. We improvised the following story in a warm up session and each wrote our own version, using the original story as a prompt.

THE AMULET

There was a house with a huge loose dog.... when an explosion erupted cast by a Mage of immemorial worlds... He was attacked by a sniper holding a bazooka .... which missed the dog by inches.... Galrog, the Mage, informed his officers that the dog had run away with the amulet and was being chased by his arch enemy the sniper..... The dog's master stood waiting for the sniper to return with the amulet.... which had been missing from the museum since the dark times rolled in.

Realising the significance of the opening line to the direction the story would take, we came up with the following opening lines....

- *The amulet of immense power was held in the mouth of a slobbering dog.*
- *'The Amulet's been stolen.'*
- *'We've located the ancient amulet!'*
- *No-one knew who the hero would be, but they didn't expect it to be the dog.*
- *The chaos began with a nondescript house.*

This one sentence collective story warm up, triggered variations, where we realised that mashing genres had its place, and from every beginning there are infinite story variations. Most of these examples are starting points for longer stories and there was no lack of ambition for epic storytelling from this group.

Cherise said: *'I want to write a Young Adult / Future Dystopia, in which an Amulet has been stolen and needs to be recovered by the hero who places himself in danger to retrieve it.'*

THE DARK AGES
By C.R. Mallett

As the war began, the dark ages rolled in, hiding in an abandoned house in the middle of a busy town centre. Nobody knew of it, until my only friend came to me and placed a strange fire red object by my dirty, bare feet.

'What's this, Bruno?' I asked. The house shook as an explosion hit the town centre, and troops emerged from all directions, armed with the new 'sniper 600's'. *Were they looking for someone?* I thought, *as I'm no use to them.* I am a lonely man with nothing but a damaged, abandoned house for shelter, wearing rags that smell of wet dog.

One trooper shouted, 'We know you're in there. Surrender now!'

Were they talking to me? I'm the only person here. At least I thought I was. I peered through the upstairs window holding this random object in my hand and before I knew it, the sniper was firing bazookas at me. As I fell onto the floor, Bruno picked up the object and ran away.

'No. Come back here,' I shouted.

Usually, he listens to me but today he left me stranded. 'Some friend, huh!' I told myself.

I looked up to see guns pointed at my face and men dressed in shiny metal suits, with an assortment of wires on show. They looked like robots.

'Sir we command you stand with your hands in the air,' the commander ordered; the number on his front identified him as 080.

'Please,' I begged. 'I haven't done anything wrong. What do you want from me?'

He stared at me with an emotionless look as I lifted myself from the dusty ground and was struck in the face....

THE DOG

By T. Kitching

'Run! Run! Get to the town of Plascill give it to Grayton!'

The grey Weimaraner charged away from his master as fast as he could, navigating the well-known streets. Though he found it hard to breath with the mystical amulet clenched tightly between his teeth, he knew now that it was the only thing that could end this war. Making his way in and out of the quiet back lanes, he came to the giant iron gates of the Town Hall; not much further now; through the forest and then on to Plascill. Walking cautiously, knowing that the enemy would be close guarding the forest, he used his acute sense of smell and determined that the time was right to make a run for it, across the court yard to the forest.

A loud bang made his ears ring, then came the explosion followed by the smoke and flying debris. He tried not to slow, focusing on the forest edge there before him.

'Get Him!!!' The command came from the balcony of the Town Hall. Galrogg the Mage sounded both furious and agitated as the dog slipped out of sight and into the forest on his way to Plascill, to end the war.

FROM THE SNIPER'S POINT OF VIEW

By Amy Kitching

I have a job to do, the Master has commanded it. I just never thought I'd have to kill my only friend, but he brought it on himself; taking the amulet like he did. He should have known Master would not stand for such a betrayal. The amulet was his, even though he stole it from the museum; but that was not for me to question.

THE EXPLOSION

By Joe Ryan

Something was silently approaching the Austrian country manor. All directions surrounded. A clink as a grenade hit the brickwork, followed by a screaming bang. A dog was blown away in the shock wave; it entered the burning house and emerged with a golden, shiny amulet around its neck as SS officers emerged like ants to fight off the attackers. The dog was lost in the chaos, moving to another location it knew too well

AMULET STORY

By Jack Heslop

It's funny how a bit of metal on a chain can cause so much destruction and chaos. Not even something practical like a key or a lanyard, mind you, but a six-hundred-year-old bit of tat that looks like something the most down market New Age health shop would keep out the back.

It was, however, kept in the knicker drawer of an ageing spinster and her lonely, nondescript house, the last lingering remnant of a street that had been otherwise demolished decades before. Now only buses between towns passed, and it stood as a mole on the face of acres of farmland.

After the old dear had passed and her distant relatives had vacuumed up all the most obviously valuable matter, the amulet remained in its drawer, bereft even of knickers.

That was, until a magician, a mangy dog, and a cigar-chomping psychopath with a bazooka showed up. (Most of my stories, you'll find, either begin or end with a cigar-chomping psychopath.)

POEMS FROM THE GUILDHALL

Another favourite warm-up was inspired by a tour of the Guildhall by the Mayor and Councillor Gary Calver. Hearing stories of its history, we wrote collective poems adding one line each, but blind, like a game of consequences. Here's what you do:

You write a title on the bottom of a page. You write the first line at the top of the page and fold it over, leaving the title visible at the bottom of the page. Pass it to the person on your right and they add a line in response to the title, fold it over and pass it on. When you get your poem back, you add the final line. It is surprisingly effective. Here is a sample, which we used as an editing exercise in a subsequent session.

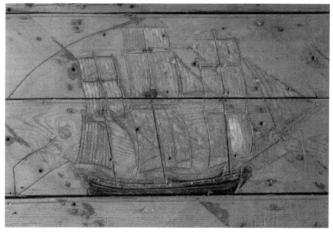

Graffiti etched into the wood panelling of the walls in the former Gaol of Harwich Guildhall. Photo by John Theobald.

THE JAIL ROOM

Darkness.
The echo of slamming doors fills the room
Surrounded by the Ghosts of past victims.
Many hours in the jail of my own making
My knife is the only thing I have now
To etch my history into the walls.
A life in etchings and despair

WITCHMAN

The Witchman stared precariously.
Why was his name on the wall?
Carved with what crude implements,
he did not know.
A Witch hunt?
A spell that ends, then begins?
A forgotten person;
But always remembered
As a name on a wall

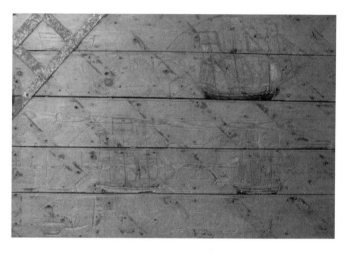

Graffiti etched into the wood paneling of the walls in the former cells of Harwich Guildhall. Photo by John Theobald

TRAPPED

How do I get out; can I escape?
There is no light in the darkness,
now I am trapped.
Hours of torture tied up
Suffocating darkness filled my world.
Claustrophobic walls built in my mind.
I can free my spirit by drawing on the walls.
That is how I escape.

THE CONDEMNED

Condemned by Man. By life. By me.
Their last goodbyes have broken free
To the narrow street outside,
But soon we're lost for all of time.
The heart within
Was unmistakable, though dread
Sat dark inside, it's knife to the wall
Compressed in the forgotten room,
You are afraid, alone.

JAIL

Punishment.
Dark and cold
like bare stone floors
with little food to console the incarcerated.
What crime was committed?
Who knows or cares
Now that only shadows dance, the cries
Long silenced on some winter day.
Doomed, your fate decided by others,
The warmth of suns will never come again.
It is a cold story.

The Town Crier's Bell, from The Guildhall, Harwich.
From a photograph by John Theobald

THE BELL

Rings across the dull, grey ocean
Every chime feeling like an hour.
Now, a silhouette before the coloured glass.
It once rang out across the land
So loud that all would stand.
From the dull chime of the crier's hand,
It rings still, mournfully in the mist.

DARK ROOMS OF HISTORY

The sins and hopes accumulated like treasured
objects
Holding secrets, stories to tell.
If these walls could speak, what would they
say?
Who made these carvings within the rooms of
our past?
Someone must have been here.
Was there no light or just darkness?
The prisoners of war brought to light
eventually.
The past maybe in the past but still defines us.

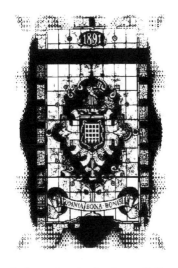

Stained glass window, 1891, in the Council Chamber, Harwich
Guildhall. From an original photograph by John Theobald

The glass bears the inscription:
Omnia Bona Bonis
To the good, all things are good

STAINED GLASS

He peered through the stained-glass window
As though he was stuck in time
Shimmering light of blue gold and green
Stain the floor when the sun hits just right.
Coloured stories depicting the past.
Soft and beautiful, genius visible.

Portrait of Alderman William Groom from the Council Chamber, Harwich Guildhall. Mayor of Harwich on eight occasions between 1877 and 1902
From a photograph by John Theobald

MAYOR GENERATIONS

The Golden Chain
Hangs heavy on their necks
Now looking down on our present.
Bright colours and past generations,
Become the mantle of the town.
The silver seal of history
Weighs heavily
On high, the power line electrified
Forever down in time.

PICTURE PROMPTS

Pictures prompted many stories and poems. In our warm-ups, we used pictures to prompt opening lines and realised that the first line sets the tone for what is to follow: the theme, genre and voice of the story; here are some opening lines from a picture prompt of an old boat grounded at low tide:

- *It was the storm which took me by surprise...*
- *They had abandoned the old boat and run away....*
- *It happened so quickly; in the blink of an eye it was gone....*
- *The police found the missing boat last night...*

- *They feared the worst....*
- *Wrecked and sunk by the scumbags...*
- *It was an act of mutiny...*
- *A dispute over the ransom, most likely...*
- *In its disrepair and isolation, it had the feel of a ruined chapel, pregnant with old prayers.*

And our one sentence story from the picture went like this ...

The ship creaked with age.
It seemed like it was abandoned
Whatever mariner had once loved it, that love was now gone.
I wonder if it can tell us the love story it contains?
What was a once beautiful boat, loved and cherished, now remains stranded,
Forever, in eternity.

After lunch there is often an energy slump, so, we would go for a brisk walk around the historic old town of Harwich, with a task which related back to the aims of the session. It started with conversations to get to know each other better and to develop the habit of asking questions. Then we took our own picture prompts. One of my favourites is *'eye spy'* in which you take each letter of your name and find an image to represent it. We progressed to images taken through the eyes of our characters and to images which were curious or demanded a response from us.

The simple image of a tree stump triggered a number of poems and stories.

Here's what Terri said about it:
It's amazing what you can get from a picture prompt, for a poem or a story. With one of the pictures of an old tree stump taken in the church yard near the Guildhall, we were tasked to come up with an idea which could be a base to tell a story or poem... we decided that the stump could still have a use, even though it was no longer a fully-grown tree. I imagined children and how free their imaginations are, and what they might use the stump for when playing.

IMAGINATION

By T. Kitching

A throne for a King, a racing car;
The top of a mountain, a cookie jar.
Rapunzel seated way up high;
A dragon flying through the sky.
A jockey who's in a fast paced race;
An astronaut taking a first step in space.
A big steel drum, a statue's base,
The beginning and the end of a race.
A ship on which to hoist a sail,
A brand new friend to tell a tale.
A place where imagination grows,
Where you'll end up...no one knows.

THE LITTLE STUMP THAT COULD

By T Kitching

On a wet and windy night, a Hedgehog was looking for a home.

In the first garden, she came across a pile of leaves.

'This looks good for a home,' she thought. As she got closer she could see a pair of green eyes and a wet black nose.

It was a Fox!

'You can't come in here, I found it first.

This will keep me safe; this is my home,' said the Fox.

The Hedgehog moved to the second garden where there stood a fine tall tree.

'This would be good for a home,' she thought, but as she got closer she could see through the branches a bushy grey tail.

It was a Squirrel!

'You can't come in here, this tree is mine and it is my home,' said the Squirrel.

The Hedgehog moved to the third garden. It was overgrown but she could see something at the bottom.

She walked closer and could see it was an old tree stump.

She moved closer still, and could see an opening at its base.

She went even closer, and scurried inside.

The strong roots from what was once a fully grown tree had made tunnels and caves that went deep into the ground.

The Hedgehog said, 'This will keep me safe; this little stump could be my home'.

During the night, the storm got worse; the wind howled and the rain fell, but Hedgehog slept soundly in her new home.

The next morning, the sun came out and it was a beautiful day. The Hedgehog went to check that Squirrel was okay.

She found Squirrel next to its tree. The tree had blown down in the storm!

He said, 'It was a beautiful home; it was so big and strong but not strong enough.'

'You could come and live with me in my stump' said Hedgehog 'It has plenty of room.'

'Yes please' said Squirrel.

So Hedgehog and Squirrel went to check that Fox was ok.

'Gone! Gone! Gone!' said the Fox. 'It was so beautiful but the wind blew it away'.

'You can come live with us in our little stump; it has plenty of room,' said the Hedgehog.

'Yes, you can!' said Squirrel.

'Thank you,' said Fox.

That night as Hedgehog, Squirrel and Fox were falling asleep the Little Stump thought to itself...

'LOOK at ME!!

I thought I had no more use after I was cut down to a stump...

But now I see that I'm still of use to these three.

No longer am I just earth and wood...

I am the Little Stump that Could!'

THE STUMP

by Tapiwa MacHin

I wilted in the winter.
Bloomed and shared the beauty of my flowers
in the summer.
But now I'm just a stump that is cut with no
purpose.
If only I could get a little water to live and be
green again.
My roots are the only thing that is keeping me
alive.
Wishing I served another purpose.
Now I'm just a stump that serves no purpose

THE FOREST HOME

By C.R. Mallett

I'm just a little stump
I used to be a tree
But I guess storms just don't like me
Or I would still be

It took me by surprise
I'm sure next time I'll fight.
No more storms will damage me,
For I will make sure I shine bright

I may just be a stump
but I have more purpose than you know
for now I can be many things
that will make people's faces glow

The following picture prompts were taken in Harwich on a post lunch walk.

The writers took photographs of images which represented a letter in their name.

Amy said: 'I liked how creative we had to be to get our names in pictures.'

The writers decided to use some of the images they took, to tell of an incident from the point of view of characters they had created for a different exercise.

Matilda, her pet monkey Tallulah and brother Andrew joined the group as recurring characters in many exercises.

Their complete story, *The Mysterious Islanders,* is told in synopsis, in the *Memory Lane* chapter of this book.

THE SEAFRONT

Amy Kitching
(Andrew's Point of View)

I needed to stay away. I wanted this to work, to be part of civilisation again and lead a normal adult life. So at first I kept away but it called me, the waves, and the sand. The smell pulled me closer, that briny, salty aroma. The water was too cold for a swim, so I sat on the sand dune and watched the waves. I had hated the sea for what it had taken; my parents and my childhood. It feels strange now to miss the life I had hated so much. I sat for hours watching the waves; the sky a reddish purple readying itself for the night. And for the first time I longed for that beautiful cage, and in my mind I will never be free from the sea.

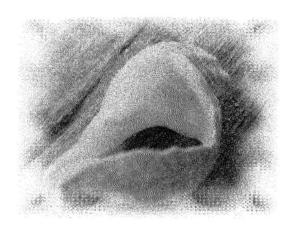

THE SHELL

C.R. Mallett

Matilda's Memory

I've got this shell; such a beautiful little thing, the way the swirls fall into one another. I found it in a rock pool when I was a little girl, helping Tallulah save some trapped fish.

The sun was beaming that day, the rays of light creating a beautiful rainbow across the water. Something I will never forget.

It must have been an old hermit crabs home; hope he didn't miss it when I took it. It's so pretty, I kept it with all the things I found during the years I spent on that island; but the shell was always my favourite.

I lost it once and I cried, but Andrew helped me look for it. It was in such a silly place; under my bed the whole time! I thought I'd looked there but I mustn't have looked properly.

I know it must seem ridiculous as it was only a shell, but it is the shell I found with my only friend. One of the few memories I hold close from my adventures with Tallulah that I could salvage from the boat Andrew built before it got burnt.

I will keep this shell forever.

Maybe one day I will be reunited with Tallulah again on the Island, and I can show her that she has never been, nor ever will be, forgotten.

OBJECT PROMPTS

Another favourite prompt is a tray of random objects which I have collected over the years. I asked the writers what relevance an object on the tray might have for their character.

Amy said:
I saw the compass and could imagine Andrew being interested in knowing where he was going. He had been lost and needed something which would let him know where he was. He had lost his parents and been protector of his sister and aunt. He had lost his childhood and sense of himself. The compass was therefore of great value to him and a metaphor for his loss.

THE COMPASS

By Amy Kitching

I had never seen a compass, until I reached the mainland. But now it is part of my life. When we finally reached civilisation, I thought my life would begin again; that the island would become a distant dream, but instead the urban world became my nightmare. I was trapped in a society I was no longer a part of, separated from my little sister. I couldn't do it; I had become my aunt, torn between civilisation and the wilds. I had to go back. I was older, wiser and prepared to go back to the place I had wished so much to be free from. With my compass in hand, I had made my decision.

THE ROCKING HORSE

C.R Mallett

Matilda's Memory

Andrew carved this with his bare hands. Being so young he knew I needed some comfort, so he gathered the supplies and carved me this rocking horse.

Before I met Tallulah, the rocking horse was my joy, my comfort! I never felt alone; he was my friend.

It really felt like I was riding a real horse, although back then, I never knew what a real horse really was. But Andrew used to share his stories.

My brother used to push me around when I

got upset; he would comfort me just like you would expect a big brother to comfort his little sister.

He was my hero!

Every time I sat upon this horse my imagination went wild; I even imagined it had wings! It took me to all the places I could of ever have dreamed of but could never visit. It felt so real.

Although I was very young, I think of this rocking horse and I smile because I just know!

So, I hand this rocking horse down through generations in the hope that it can also bring you the joy, laughter & comfort it once brought to me.

.

POETRY

INTRODUCTION

By Jack Heslop

I first began writing poetry regularly during my teenage years, after discovering Sylvia Plath and Anne Sexton, two American poets from the mid-20th-century who wrote a lot about their emotional lives. I've always loved poetry, having read Shakespeare in school and enjoyed his sonnets, but before Plath and Sexton I always felt that composing poetry was beyond me. What those writers showed me was that the stuff of your everyday life and thoughts, even their ugliest aspects, can be used to make beautiful poems.

These days my favourite poet is Philip Larkin, the grumpy old man of English poetry who, inspired by the melancholic poems of 19th-century writer Thomas Hardy, wrote a lot about mid-20th-century England with a bracingly cynical yet sympathetic voice. To this day I still know all the words to possibly his most famous work, 'This Be the Verse'.

As for my own poetry I try to write on a number of subjects, and have found that as you grow as a poet, even as an amateur hobbyist like me, your work becomes dominated by your own distinctive voice as it grows from your particular worldview. Just as the painter doesn't merely re-create the world but injects it with his own special consciousness, so the poet cannot merely describe. If perspective is the soul of painting, voice is the soul of poetry.

INSIDE ST. NICHOLAS CHURCH, HARWICH

A Sonnet by Jack Heslop

A painted offering of stone
behind a great altar, beside
the plaques that give the Words. The throne
is glimpsed within this place, the hides
of souls its cushioning, its arms
and legs golden. What ancient charms
can still be seen among the pews
and high inside the organ's flues
are stepping out, again to see
the faithful come to kneel, to plea.
The nave is packed with tourists now.
The portrait of Moses with God's
tablets - ten rules inscribed for how
a life should play - looks on, at odds.

FROM A BENCH IN THE VILLAGE OF WEELEY

By Jack Heslop

A bench in shadows on a small apron
of land beside a crematorium
and church. The light seductive on
its ancient way to travelers,
the dappled ken is cool and warm at once,
and strangely unperturbed by passing cars.
A rambler sits and prays a while hence,
hands on knees and voice as quiet as dusk.
The age of lengthy meditations past,
he knows he'll have to stand and walk again,
but as the fleeting moment lasts
an old and silent spell will greet his lips:
'Vanish the fleeting joy in winter graves,
a little time in dappled April saves.'

WORTHY OF YOUR LOVE

A prose poem by Jack Heslop

I am the Unknown in this family. My name is such-and-such a name, fairly standard, welding me to the tree from which we all spring like branches. Or maybe the correct metaphor is leaves, each person a lush green leaf in the opening days of Spring, studded with raindrops like military medals. I, however, am a brown leaf with no medals, dry as a funeral director's wit. Accustomed, it seems, to my own cycle of seasons, divorced from the cycle of the leaves around me. My Autumns and Winters are perversely long, where theirs are nothing compared to an almost perpetual Spring, ending in a perfect Summer.

This bothers me less now than it once may have, because although the surface differences might burn themselves onto my eyes like shattering revelations, I remember that all us leaves are fed by the same tree. That beneath our skins and even deeper than our bones is a simple, essential idea that links us all, one to the other.

This idea is that we are humans, a kind of animal, one of the kinds that Noah gathered in the ark and Charles Darwin traced the evolution of. As individuals we might be driven by any number of fears and desires. We might be grotesque, monstrous, carnival-esque repositories of cruelty and hate, fit only for the freak shows of the human soul.

We might be love itself distilled into a human form, set walking in this world to bring forth gardens from the hardest soils, a constant joy to those we know and many we've yet to meet. More likely, we are somewhere in-between.

And that alone is worthy of your love.

PARK RUN

By Amy Kitching

I may not be the fastest,
But I am here...

I may not be the strongest,
But I am here...

I may not be the fittest,
But I am here...

I am determined,
That's why I'm here.

CATS

By T. Kitching

You've added to our family
In your own hairy way

Growing as we too grow
Sharing each and every day

You've shared in our emotions
The highs and the lows

You've been shouted at and loved
Sometimes stepped upon; heaven knows

Your purrs and gentle meows
Show us contentment and your love

We're sure that you were sent to us
From angels up above

We like to call you family
You fine four legged friends

But one more crap found in his shoe
He swears that it's the end!

VISUAL POEMS

By K. Ngai

Poems come in all shapes and sizes.

Poems which make a picture are often referred to as Concrete poems, sometimes Visual or Shape poems. K. Ngai expresses his thoughts and ideas in pictures, practicing the art of Manga style Japanese character drawings. During the 12 weeks of the Creative Writing Project, K's responses were deeply imbedded in this tradition. More of his character drawings can be seen in '*The Omega Retribution*' in the *Short Story* chapter of this book. He worked in partnership with Jack Heslop to develop a narrative around Manga characters, and create a visual world in which their story could be told.

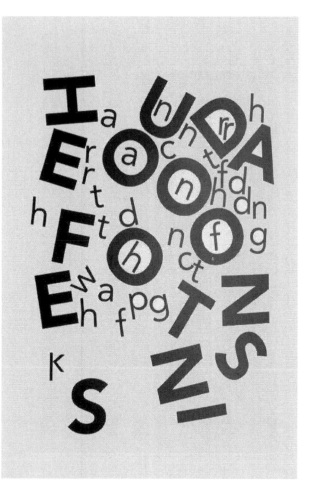

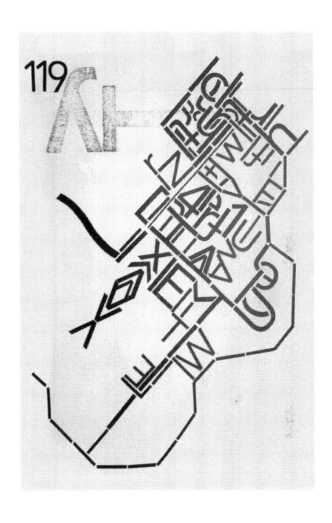

THE REDOUBT

Photograph curtesy of The Harwich Society

We spent a day at The Redoubt Fort in Harwich, which proved to be an excellent place of stories and inspiration. We were discovering, through these sessions, that creativity does not happen in a straight line, and needs to be prompted with a series of questions, curiosity, inspiration and *focused* activities; and because creativity flourishes on the edge of chaos, we need to focus ourselves also in order to avoid the chaos of overload. To begin with, we considered the senses:

Looking: What is your Point of View? Are you seeing from the outside in, or from the inside out; high on the ramparts, or low down in the moat.

Listening: If these walls could talk what secrets might you hear?

Touching the surfaces and absorbing the atmosphere and noticing the smell of wood smoke and lime washed walls and damp and *noticing* the difference between how it was then, and how it is now.

We took photo prompts of people, objects, and spaces, and began to make connections between these things to weave new stories into the fabric of this fortress, forged in the imagination of the writers and expressed through the feelings they sparked.

THE RESULT OF WAR
By C.R. Mallett

I'm here... I can see... But I can hear nothing except the pulsing of my heart trying to leap out of my chest... I'm so scared, but I'm not going to quit. All I can see are men shouting and screaming at one another, yet there is still no sound.

I see mothers holding their screaming children tightly praying for what may be one last time.

I need to help, but I can't move; I feel numb! Why do I feel numb? Soldiers are rushing towards me with bandages. Am I hurt? I feel nothing. There are men risking their lives to help me like they have nothing to lose. '*No man left behind*' was our motto: now that is loyalty.

I'm starting to feel drowsy, like I need to sleep. Why am I so tired? How do I let go of this feeling?

As I peer into the distance I see my wife Lyla; I can see her screaming out for me. She looks so terrified. But everything will be fine!

I'm here my love.

I feel my eyes close, only for a moment, but when I open them again, I can see myself lying on the floor. I look so fragile, surrounded by blood. And then I realise that I can't see my legs, let alone feel them. Is this real?

Lyla is crying. She wasn't supposed to see me this way. I hope you can forgive me. I won't leave you for I am still here!

As I walk towards her, I grasp her close.

'I'm holding your hands, but you can't feel me! Why can't you feel me? Are you numb too? You're not listening to me! Why can't you hear me? *I am not dead!*

Whilst bombs fall around us, I try to get you back inside, but you won't listen. You know it's not safe out here, yet you continue to risk your life.

Dirt fills the air as thousands of bullets hit the ground at once. There are already many injured people; blood everywhere I look. Please my love, go inside; I need you safe for our daughter. Including our unborn child. I can't lose you. Tell our kids I love them eternally. I will come home I promise; I will fight until the end just to keep you safe.

Wait? Where are you going? You're starting to fade... Please don't fade. Come back Lyla! Don't leave me!

Everything went dark for a few moments and I thought I'd lost her, but when I opened my eyes I was lying in a hospital bed. Why am I here? I can't remember anything.

All I can see are nurses rushing around me, some with tears rolling down their faces, others putting on a brave face.

So many soldiers were being rushed inside, many with open wounds, including my own. I looked down towards the end of the bed, and realise that I have no legs. The nurses have me hooked up to some machines; they managed to control the bleeding and supplied me with some more. Sounds are faintly returning and now I can hear screams of innocent people, whilst guns are blazing, planes soaring and sirens blaring.

I can hear the nurses screaming at one another about beds; 'We need more beds,' I heard one shout, whilst others were sliding tables across the floor.

I think about my daughter, Marie, hoping she is safe.

I want to speak to someone but every time I try to speak, nothing seems to come out. I just want to go home.

All around me is blood and death.

Laying here unable to move I saw a body being carried inside. They laid him on a table and I saw his face. It was Raymond, my lifetime childhood friend.

This couldn't be, I told myself, tears running down my cheeks as they covered his face with a stained red sheet. Why him? He didn't deserve this. He was only 26, and was supposed to be getting married once the war was over. And now he will never get that chance to watch the love of his life walk down that aisle to take their vow's. I was going to be best man.

I will no longer be able to walk anywhere. We all had so much to live for; but I still have my life, unlike the others, lying on that battlefield ground lifeless.

Napoleonic soldier Mannequins in the Barrack Room

FORBIDDEN LOVE
By Tapiwa MacHin

It has been over 2 years now since I lost Henry. All things have a beginning and an end; it all started to go wrong the day I moved into The Redoubt after being rescued from my country. He was the only person there for me when I was trying to adjust to all the changes and my time in need, as I was new at the refugee camp. The way he cared for me, it was like I was one of his own. Blinded by everything else that was going on, I never realised the way I felt about Henry.

The feeling was mutual. It was like the unfortunate love that started in very difficult times or situations and grew stronger as time passes. Before we knew it, we were like a couple which has been seeing each other for quite some time, without clarification of how both felt.

Before we knew it again the words I love you were already a song in our hearts, meeting in secret and at least trying to be a normal couple, since love for people of our age was forbidden till we reach a certain age. It was as if war was more important and we had to forget how to live.

Henry was a Land Army boy and I was just a normal refugee in rags. My name is Alice West and this is for my son who is probably going to grow up without both parents. I lost my Henry after he was sent out to war, without being trained like any other soldiers.

He died for our sins since the night our secret came out through the well of no secrets at The Redoubt, the conversation of our intimacy echoing away to the wrong ears; his superior; although we thought it was all whispers. It was not the first time the superior had warned Henry about being close to women even if it was all innocent and out of his caring heart.

But this time it was different. The moment

the superior heard about our intimacy, he was ready to transfer me to another location God knows where, but my Henry pleaded with his superior to be relocated in my place. Henry was sent to war and he never made it back and the rest of the soldiers were back but him. His belongings were not even brought back to The Redoubt like other soldiers, as a sign of honour and respect.

But now I have got a disease which doctors cannot cure because no one knows what the disease is.....

THE FORT

By Amy Kitching

The mouth was wide and intimidating, in contrast to its narrow eyes. Suffocated by its unblinking stare, I shuddered feeling even smaller then I already was. I imagined a booming voice calling at me and echoing through the maze like chambers with its walls peeling like rotten flesh. Even though the room itself was small and unremarkable, the face with its alien expression encapsulated me there. I wondered then who else had succumbed to its ominous presence. I looked away, and then still feeling its life like gaze; Sweat began to pour over my fragile frame. As the walls themselves brushed against my clammy skin, I wanted so much to escape the encroaching room. I tightened my eyes and begged for my mother to come save me, my cries spawned into wails as the realisation that this was all but a twisted nightmare of a once hopeless child.

I had awoken with my head slumped into the stool next to me. Tears streamed from my blood shot eyes as the haze of the dream slowly wore off. My throat dry and itchy; I reached up to the bar side for the one thing that could save me; my next drink. I don't have to look around to know that their eyes are on me, studying my every move. I try to keep calm, but I'm sweating and the image of that place is bored into the back of my eyes. My head ached as the deafness of the room hit me. The smell of stale ale and cigar smoke settled on my tongue. I can taste it, my disgrace; they all knew it too. The white feather I wore as a sign of cowardice was one I earned so easily.

Carronades on the Gun Deck

WRITTEN INSIDE THE REDOUBT

By Jack Heslop

The earth is always claiming,
always taking back that which
we leave behind. Windows erupting
with foliage, daisies skirting
the centre mound. A stitch
in history to earth is just
more ground to seize and plant anew,
the turning of the world, the light,
making even bricks their own,
glass a new species of rose.

Radar equipment in Rebow Room

T. Kitching writes:
Whilst on a visit to the Redoubt Fort in Harwich
we were tasked with walking around and taking
pictures of things that captured our imagination
and that may help to provoke a story, character
or poem from within us. We made connections
between the images to write a story.

With the uniform, I could imagine a sea Captain;
with the radar equipment I could envision the
radio rooms during the war. But the ventilation
grate for me was the key... what could be hidden
in there and how many people would walk by this
unassuming hiding place?

Uniform from a Merchant Marine

CAPTAIN GEORGE MARSHAM

By T. Kitching

I'd been a Sea Captain for many years, after making my way through the ranks. My first commission was on the HMS Good Hope; she led convoys to and from docks, carrying food, ammunition and other supplies to where they were needed.

Due to injury, I now work in the radio rooms tracking ships and sending, receiving and intercepting messages; well not personally!
On one secret mission, I had to become a

landlubber, based at the Redoubt Fort in Harwich. It was all hush, hush! Certain that one of the men was a spy, I had to watch the men like hawks to see if I could find the culprit hiding codes in the wall grates. Can't have the secrets from our communications room getting out and into the wrong hands. This is a bloody war after all.

I decided to continue my story on a different path when tasked with connecting the pictures to create a different form of story-telling.

To continue from Captain George's story, I decided to write a letter from the wife of the supposed spy to help explain what was actually going on. I imagined that the secret messages in the grates were from a husband to a wife; both working in the fort yet unable to see each other. So they passed intimate notes in a code which they had devised in their childhood.

With Captain George's story, we have the setup of a suspected traitor whom he must find; then, with the letter, we know that we have found him but it's not as Captain George thought.

Ventilation Grill

THE LETTER

By T. Kitching

My Dearest Darling John,

It has now been 6 months, 12 days and 9 hours since I saw you last; how my heart longs to beat next to yours again. I will try to come and see you next month, as long as I can get leave to do so. I hope you are well and eating properly and that you received the parcel I sent last week. I hope you are wearing the jumper I got for you to help keep you warm and to protect you from the cold and damp.

I have sent the letter to the Admiralty,

as you requested, to try to explain the situation we now find ourselves in. Who would have thought that a few notes in a reminisced childish code could get you in so much trouble? I was reprimanded and had rest room duties for 3 months; you have been locked in the cells by Captain Marsham all this time awaiting your trial.

I'm still trying to find out where Dickie Broom has been billeted; to get him to confirm our code from childhood.

You are no traitor to your country, you are not a disgrace.

I can't bear to think of you in that pitiful white washed room they call a prison. It makes me angry how they have twisted everything; your sweet and innocent letters to me are now your reason for being there.

Keep your chin up my love. Once Dickie is found, they will know that you are no spy. To think that your old teacher from Oxford could be our saviour!

I will have to stop here as tears are filling my eyes in the hopes of seeing you again soon.

Love as always,
Your loving May xxx

MEMORY LANE

T. Kitching writes:

We were asked to use the senses to evoke our memories; for me; smells bring back lots of vivid childhood memories. We then had to put them into a written form; I chose poetry.

GERMOLENE AND AUNTIE DOT

By T. Kitching

The smell of Germolene reminds me of you
A small cut, a grazed knee
Your white hair sparkled from the window
behind you
Your chair sometimes rocked free
The small cupboard where you kept the tiny
blue and white tin
The photo of your mother black and white
made the pink ointment all the brighter
The Germolene felt as smooth as your warm
touch
Your smile is there before me when I think of
you;
After the aroma of Germolene which arouses
the sense of you.

BOILED SWEETS OF GRANDAD EAGLE
By T. Kitching

Waiting for you to return, arms opened wide.
Not for a hug but for you to be mugged.
Boiled sweet surprise,
your pockets we'd rummage through.
Then would come the hugs
and the mint kisses too.

Not all of the memories were based on real life experiences. The following memories are from the fictional characters which Amy and Cherise had created in one of our earlier sessions. These characters sparked a series of short pieces, plus a synopsis for a much longer work: *The Mysterious Islanders*, as well as Cherise's *Stories for Children*.

THE MYSTERIOUS ISLANDERS

Synopsis

By Amy Kitching and C.R. Mallett

When Matilda receives a mysterious tweet, she is forced to remember a past she has long forgotten. She is finally ready to accept her past and forgive herself for what she believes she did to her brother and aunt

At the age of two, Matilda is shipwrecked on an island with her older brother Andrew and their Aunt Maude. They survive for 8 years, and Matilda's best friend is her pet Monkey, Tallulah. As the years pass, however, Aunt Maude gradually loses her mind.

Andrew has built a boat and is desperate to find their way back to civilisation, but on the night they are ready to leave, Aunt Maude disappears leaving no trace of her whereabouts. Andrew persuades Matilda that they must leave and start a new life wherever they end up.

When they find the mainland, as minors, they are separated and placed in care, and Matilda realises that her years on the Island were very different to the world she now has to face. She has travelled from Paradise to the realities of a harsh and bullying world.

Despite her struggle to adapt, she makes a new life for herself as a successful business woman running garden centres, where her Island skills are valuable, and she begins to forget about her time on the Island. But she never quite forgets her brother Andrew, although accepting that she may never see him again.

Meanwhile, Matilda does not know that Andrew has returned to the island as an adult, and holds a dark secret.

On her birthday, she gets a Tweet, supposedly from her pet monkey Tallulah. Shocked and intrigued in equal measure, she replies and is sent dates and directions of how to get back to the Island; the message says that Tallulah will meet her at the port.

When she gets to the Island, she discovers her brother Andrew, now living as a wild man.

He tells her the secret...

PART TWO

What really happened on the island and to Aunt Maude? Did Andrew kill her because Maude wouldn't agree to leave, and tried to burn the boat? Then did he make Matilda believe that she had caused their Aunt to drown?

Andrew resents that Matilda has built a new life. It soon becomes clear that she is now in danger, alone on the Island, knowing Andrew's dark secret and not able to escape....

ANDREWS'S MEMORIES OF THE ISLAND

By Amy Kitching

I was ten when we were shipwrecked on the island; me, my sister and aunt had somehow survived but our parents were gone. There was no time to grieve. My aunt made it clear we should only think of our survival. It was hard work and as Matilda was too young to help, it was up to me and Aunt Maude to build the shelter, find food and clean water. I was about twelve years old when the bungalow was fully completed; it was safe and kept us alive. But I hated it. I often argued with Aunt Maude about escaping the island and going home. Her reasoning was that we didn't know where we were and Matilda was too young. I think that's why I began to resent my sister. As the years passed I thought of ways to leave and planned to build a raft. I searched the island for materials and dreamed of escaping, but even though I wanted to go, I couldn't leave them.

My sister had become a wild child with her pet monkey Tallulah causing havoc and my aunt had become a shell; she walked around talking to herself in whispers. I was worried for them both.

I was sixteen when the raft was completed and it was the worst thing I have ever done.

THE BEACH

C. R. Mallett

Matilda's Memory

I love walking along the beach, one footstep in front of the other, feeling the grains of sand between my toes. Ocean waves that come crashing down one after another, whilst that cool sea breeze flows through my hair.

I feel like that little girl again, the girl who could roam the beaches all day, doing whatever she wanted, until the sun began to set.

Flashbacks come flooding back. I watch children building sandcastles, laughing, smiling and chasing one another.

It reminds me of myself and Tallulah.

I miss her. I wonder how she is doing now? I would love to go back and be that care free child again enjoying life. But I can't. Everyone has to grow up and I am part of reality now; I work for money.

I built a business growing exotic plants and although many people love them, I still find it hard to make friends.

Not many people like me: I will always be called 'that girl from the island,' just because we have a different outlook on life.

All I know about is survival, but nobody understands that. I never get much chance to walk along the beach now, but whenever I get free time I will visit, just so I can feel like the child I once was.

But the question is; do we really need to grow up? Even adults can enjoy the beach, because we are all the same children at heart that we always were.

It's your choice to let the child out.
Memories last a lifetime,
And that's the beauty of a beach.

THE BLOSSOM TREE

C.R. Mallett

Matilda's Memory

I remember a very long time ago, a Blossom tree; how those little flower petals would bloom. They looked beautiful.

I never knew what kind of tree it was, until I found one on the mainland. I remember waking up one morning to the sun beaming so bright through my bedroom window. I got up to take a look outside and all I could see was a blanket of white petals falling one by one. Andrew smiled and said it looked like snow.

'What's snow?' I asked him, and he told me.

Every night after that, I sat at my bedroom window waiting for it to snow. I wished for it every evening in the hope that it would happen, but it never did. I felt disappointed but that feeling soon passed. So instead as each year went by, I waited for spring to arrive just so that I could watch those soft petals grow and bloom into something beautiful.

I used to sit by the window in our bungalow waiting for the petals to fall, and when they did, I went outside just to dance in the sun's rays and the snowing petals, laughing. Catching those tiny petals with my hands feeling their soft texture brush against my skin whilst they got tangled in my hair was a magical feeling.

Aunt Maude used to stand by the door watching me, her smile was enough to brighten the darkest of days. She used to say to me:

'Never let what you can't see interfere with how you see the world, and you will do many wonderful things. Stay humble and happy.' How right she was.

I soon forgot about the snow, and I focused on that one tree.

And that my sweet grandchildren, is why we have a blossom tree in the back yard.

When you are feeling lost and losing hope, just go and sit under that tree. Watch the little blossom petals fall around you, and I promise you that you will not be lost anymore, but be smiling to yourself.

Nature is Beautiful. It can do so many things.

STORIES FOR CHILDREN

The Adventures of Tallulah and Matilda

By C. R. Mallet

When Amy and I came up with the story of The Mysterious Islanders, featuring a young girl shipwrecked with her brother and aunt, there were so many ideas, that I decided to write some children's stories based on Matilda and her pet monkey, Tallulah, who became her best friend on the island.

They did everything together, as best friends do, from fishing, playing hide and seek, and much more! I was inspired to write these stories because I have two young children and I wanted to tell them stories where they could picture what was happening and use their imagination.

I wrote these three stories based on what I thought my children would find fun and interesting to listen to: having friends, being kind and helpful, all traits which are important to growing children.

These are stories for my children and I hope they can share in Matilda and Tallulah's Adventures.

TALLULAH'S BIRTHDAY

By C.R. Mallett

Do you know what day it is today?
It's a very special day!

It's Tallulah's Birthday!

Matilda was planning a surprise birthday party, so in the morning, whilst Tallulah was still sleeping Matilda snuck out!

As she went downstairs she saw her brother.

'Andrew, Please could you help me with these invitations' Matilda whispered,

'Of course I can, who are they for?' Andrew replied.

So Matilda had a long think of who she could invite to the party!

She invited Miss Cara the Crab, Mr. Logan The Lizard, Mr. Kasey The Kangaroo, Little Lily Lion, and last of all Alfie the Anteater.

'I'd better go and hand these invitations out to all Tallulah's friends!' Matilda thought to herself, and off she went to hand them all out!

Just as Matilda left, Tallulah got out of bed. Meanwhile Matilda had handed out the invitations to all of Tallulah's friends making sure they could keep it a secret!

When that was done, Matilda went around the island looking for some stuff she could us as decorations, but Tallulah saw her.

Matilda quickly scurried away!

This left Tallulah feeling very upset, so she went to find someone else to play with.

She saw Cara the crab...but Cara hid away! So Tallulah went to see if she could find one of her other friends.

Then she saw Logan the lizard. He ran away too!

So Tallulah went to see if she could find one of her other friends.

She found Kasey the Kangaroo, but as soon as he saw her he hopped away very quickly.

So Tallulah went to see if she could find one of her other friends.

She found Little Lily Lion, who also ran away.

So Tallulah went to see if she could find one of her other friends.

Last but not least she found her good buddy Alfie the Anteater…but he also ran away from her!

This made Tallulah very sad.

Back at home everything was ready for Tallulah's birthday party! All of her friends were there waiting for her to arrive.

But Tallulah didn't go home!

Matilda started to get worried. 'I hope she isn't upset with us for running away. I'd better go and look for her,' she said.

So Matilda went to look for her friend.

'Where would Tallulah go?' She thought to herself. Then Matilda remembered the banana tree, so she scurried off!

Matilda found Tallulah and they both walked home together!

Just as Tallulah opened the gate she heard:

'Surprise! Happy Birthday Tallulah'

Tallulah started jumping up and down with excitement! 'Eeepcha Ah Ah Eep' She Squealed.

'Happy Birthday Tallulah, we would never forget your special day,' said Matilda as she gave Tallulah a big hug.

So Tallulah and all her friends danced and

danced until the sun went down, and everyone went home.

'What a day, said Matilda, as she carried Tallulah up to bed, I wonder what tomorrow will bring?'

More Adventures perhaps?

TALLULAH GOES FISHING

By C. R. Mallett

One bright sunny morning, whilst the sun was shining across the sea, Matilda and Tallulah were sitting on the beach making sandcastles.

Then all of a sudden a big wave came splish-splashing over them! Matilda got excited and went to find some shells. But instead of shells she found something else!

I wonder what it could have been?

Was it a crab?

Maybe it was some Coral?

No?

It was a small rock pool.

And inside that rock pool were some little fishes trying to escape.

Matilda called out, 'Tallulah, Tallulah, quick come look!'.

So off Tallulah went to take a look.

'I think they want to go back into the sea, Please Tallulah can we help them?' said Matilda, looking worried.

Tallulah nodded her head whilst chatting away in her own language 'Eeepcha Ah Ah Eeep'

Matilda started jumping up and down clapping her hands, smiling and asked,

'What can we use to make a net?

'Could this leaf be a net?

'No?'

'Well, what about this shell?'

'No?'

'Oh wait I know! We could weave together a net by using these vines. We'd better get started! LETS GO!'

Tallulah's job was to find a stick for the net and as she was searching for the perfect stick to use, Matilda tried to weave a net.

But she couldn't do it!

'I won't give up! I can do this,' she thought to herself, so she tried again... and again, until finally she got it right!

Matilda did a happy dance singing to herself

'I did it... I did it!'

Tallulah was at the beach sorting out her sticks as Matilda came running over waving the net around in the air.

Tallulah chose a special stick that looked like a 'Y' shape.

'Oh Tallulah, this Is perfect!' said Matilda excitedly. 'Let's put it together'.

Once they connected the net to the stick, Matilda and Tallulah hurried towards the rock pool.

'Here Tallulah, you catch the fish and I will hold this bucket,' Matilda said, grinning, and holding out the bucket they had used for sand castles. Tallulah started fishing, but it was very hard!

'Eeepcha Ah Ah Eeep' Tallulah shouted!

'WOW, you caught one! Great job Tallulah!' said Matilda, jumping up and down. Just two more left!'

Matilda put the first fish into the bucket whilst Tallulah tried to catch the rest.

Then suddenly just as Tallulah caught the last two fish, SHE SLIPPED OFF THE ROCK!

Luckily Tallulah only landed on her bottom! And the fish flew into the sky and jumped into the sea!

'We did it!' shouted Matilda whilst hugging Tallulah. 'Let's go home!'

So off home they went to get some rest before their next adventure!

TALLULAH PLAYS HIDE AND SEEK

By C.R. Mallett

Tallulah is a spider monkey. She lives on an Island with her best friend, Matilda. One day Matilda and Tallulah were very bored.

'Tallulah I'm bored,' said Matilda holding her head in her hands. Then Matilda thought of a fun game to play!

'I know Tallulah, let's play Hide and Seek! I will count and you can hide'.

Now Tallulah thought this was a great idea, so off she went to hide.

Meanwhile Matilda was still counting,

'1... 2... 3...right up to 10!'

'Ready or not here I come,' and Matilda set off in search for Tallulah.

But where was Tallulah hiding?

Matilda started looking along the beach, but Tallulah was not there!

'Oh... I wonder where she could be?' Matilda thought to herself.

So, Matilda carried on searching.

Next, Matilda searched around the banana trees. Bananas are Tallulah's favourite!

Just then Matilda jumped out and shouted 'BOO! I found you', but Tallulah was not there either!

'That's strange. Where is Tallulah?' Matilda thought to herself.

So, Matilda carried on with her search!

Matilda looked all over the island for Tallulah. She searched the bushes, then she searched the tree house. Matilda even searched the toilet! But Tallulah was not anywhere!

'WHERE ARE YOU TALLULAH?' Matilda shouted.

Matilda decided she didn't want to play this silly game anymore, so she walked.... and walked.... until finally, she was back home.

'I do not like this game,' complained Matilda. 'I think I am going to have a nice nap.'

Matilda walked up the stairs, opened her bedroom door, and went inside, mumbling to herself. Then she noticed something moving in her bed!

'Who is there?' Matilda asked quietly, but there was no answer. So Matilda tiptoed towards the bed to take a closer look, but just as she went to pull off the cover....

Tallulah jumped out and excitedly chatted 'PEEKA-BOO'.

'Tallulah, I found you!' Matilda laughed.

Matilda gave Tallulah a very big hug and said, 'you're my best friend Tallulah,' and off they went in search of something new.

'I wonder what we can play tomorrow?' said Matilda as they walked towards the beach into the sunset.

.

SHORT STORIES

INTRODUCTION

By Jack Heslop

    I've always loved short stories and relished the chance to write one for this course. When I was first discovering books my favourite author was Edgar Allan Poe, famous for such tales of terror as *The Pit and the Pendulum* and *The Fall of the House of Usher*. I like to say I was so in love with his stories that I didn't want to be *like* Poe, I wanted to *be* Poe. (Well, apart from the arranged marriage to his thirteen-year-old cousin and the alcoholism ending in death...)

    Part of what makes a Poe story special is the structure. Many were only a few pages long and had just one setting: a cellar, an old house, a pit. For the story I wrote based on the Omega character created by K, whose illustrations accompany the text, one setting wasn't going to be enough, but I did have in mind a series of fast-paced scenes each with its own distinctive setting.

These settings were a desert planet, a gas planet, a hotel on an Earth-like planet, and, of course, this being a science-fiction story, outer space. My ideas regarding the planets were guided by K's wonderful sketches of the imaginary solar system where much of the story takes place.

Continuing this theme of efficiency in storytelling, cutting out as many distractions as possible, I recalled my favourite piece of writing advice, from a list of rules for crafting short stories by the writer Kurt Vonnegut: that every single line should either reveal character or advance plot.

Every single line. When you only have a few thousand words to work with (roughly 4.6 thousand in my case, which is still a lot more than the three thousand I originally aimed for), you can't afford to ramble. The short story tests your mettle as a storyteller, and I hope you enjoy my attempt at the form.

THE LAST OMEGA

Original concept, character, story and illustrations by K. Ngai
Written by Jack Heslop

In the very distant future...

It was as if the sun had fallen from the sky, and in an explosion of metal and glass you realised that the sun was just a giant lightbulb.

Hearing the unholy din in the sky, the being known as Omega walked from his tent like a desert prophet called by the voice of his God. The tent was significantly close to a network of enormous and long-abandoned buildings that grew from the sand like dunes, at one with the skin of the desert.

He looked up to see a great mass, a spaceship large enough to support a crew of fifty, churning in the sky, growing in size as it neared the ground. For the first time in a long time he didn't know what to do, so just stood there, staring impassively at the coming destruction. His instinct for self-preservation was untroubled by the knowledge that the ship was sufficiently far away that when it crashed the blowback wouldn't affect him; maybe it could kill or maim an ordinary human being, but not Omega.

He did, however, narrow his eyes at the

immensely loud explosion. Smoke filled the scene so that it seemed as if he was in the heart of a bonfire; he remembered learning about an obscure human ritual, from the days before space exploration, when a dummy called a 'guy' would be tied to a stake and burned. As a portion of the smoke shifted he saw that this bonfire did indeed have its own guy, a still living one that was thrashing against the restraints of its chair.

Omega walked into the smoke and the flames, adjusting the nature of his body from within so that it could withstand the inferno. With access to all kinds of abandoned technology from the buildings on this planet he had improved his android circuitry to a formidable point. Reaching the chair, which was surrounded by a buffet of shattered glass and steel, he ripped the belts from their prisoner and released the latter, slinging him over his shoulder.

He carried him out of the inferno and, seeing that his tent had been blown away to Heaven knows where, changed course towards a small nearby mountain that would have some caves. Climbing in through a cave mouth with his new companion still over his shoulder, he found a dry spot on a natural bench in the rock wall and laid him down.

Like Omega, the man was six feet tall and

muscular; unlike Omega his body had run a little too fat, and more pressingly, he was missing a hand and a lower leg. Where these appendages once were there now sprouted corsages of wire that sparked and threatened to enflame. An android, like himself... Omega looked about them at the damp, dripping rock and the little reservoir formed in a channel of the floor.

Maybe he'd done the wrong thing, bringing him here. If his circuitry was old enough it might cause a reaction if contacted by water. Omega hadn't been unsure of a decision since long before he came to this planet sixty years ago.

Androids, even those who like Omega were born human and had the machinery adapted to their bodies later, could live for hundreds of years, but they weren't immortal. Eventually the circuitry rusted to a point where it couldn't be modified without replacing the core, and with a new core came a new personality. There were whole moons littered with rusted out cores - spherical computers - that were the physical remains of human (or at least humanoid) souls.

Omega, relieved from military duty largely by a lack of pressing use for his kind, had come to this planet, this solar system, to live out his days as a hermit until he either died or became useful again. When he arrived the only other planet in the system that was still inhabited was a gas planet that had scientists hovering above it in research stations, trying to learn if the radiation could be somehow harnessed and used. Now even those stations were abandoned, fixed in place until their energy depleted and they fell into the gas.

For sixty years Omega's only use to the army that had bred and nourished him was the guardianship of the lifeless desert city, its skyscrapers housing thousands of computer terminals with which eons of information could presumably be accessed. How useful such information might be when it was left to rot in the enormous carcass of an outpost Omega neither knew nor cared; it gave his hermitage an excuse. His shattered companion grabbed him by the collar of Omega's coat, his remaining hand still strong.

'You' he said. His eyes adjusted with audible technical struggling, like automatic cameras trying to focus. 'I know you. At least, I've seen you. You were, you were... You were one of US!'

'Who are you?' said Omega.

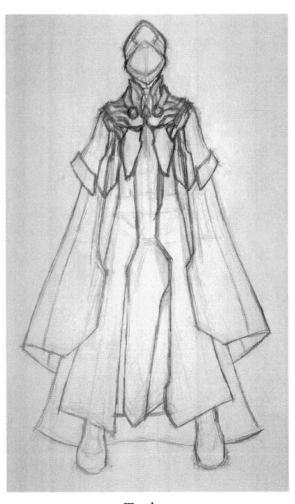

Traitor

'Super Soldier, Android Class XE092, Birth Named Zeta XVI. You... Omega?'

Omega

'That is correct. I am Omega.'

Like all of the soldiers named Omega he had a small but prominent wart on his right cheek, not far below the eye, an imperfection of the skin caused by the particular circuitry that Omegas were fitted with. 'Wow' said Zeta, laughing a little through his injury, 'I only met one of you guys once before. You were some of the real bad-asses.' The compliment was lost on Omega, who neither registered nor felt many emotions beyond mild curiosity and, so it seemed, uncertainty still.

'What happened to your ship?' said Omega.

'Sabotage. Not my ship, though. It's a cargo-class vessel. I was delivering it to a colony... I don't even know where I am. We ended up going so far off course, even hitting light speed at one point, I wouldn't be surprised if I'm not in charted space anymore.'

'You said this was sabotage?'

'You're not going to believe this, brother, but it was one of us, and not just any one of us but an ALPHA. Can you believe that? A goddamn Alpha... Jesus Christ. I don't understand it. Weren't Alphas supposed to be the most mentally stable ones? Like, not 'mentally stable', maybe, but at least not likely to go full renegade psycho...' He let out a few bloody, hacking coughs.

'Why?' said Omega

'Why what?'

'Why would an Alpha do this?'

'I don't know, brother. I honestly don't know. But before he left the ship - and he made sure to teleport off the second another ship was in range; God knows what he told them, or if he even let them live... But, yeah, like I was saying, before he left, he says to me, while I'm there dying on the floor, just waiting to see if he'll let me crawl to my chair, he says, 'take comfort, brother. You die looking at the face of God.' What do you even think he MEANT by that?' Omega confessed that (like so many things, apparently) he didn't know.

'How did he get onto your ship?'

'Like I said, not my ship. I don't control the teleporters and all that junk on those things. The people I work for, they just give me this pre-programmed vessel and tell me where to take it. I'm not even supposed to leave the main bridge. That Alpha must have, I don't know, done his research on the vessel, tapped into the transporter codes and beamed across from his own ship. I'll tell you this, though, I put up a fight. He was planning to just kill me and go back to his ship, I can tell, but I gave him a run for his money and he had to improvise. Not that it did me much good in the end...

Omega had removed his coat and used it as a blanket to cover Zeta, having first stopped his wires from sparking. 'Did you lose your hand and leg in the crash?' Zeta trembled, as if suddenly remembering. 'No... He took them. We were fighting and he just... Tore them from me. He knew what he was doing. He sought out the joints and just tore. He turned off the pain receptors first so I wouldn't feel anything, though I think that was just because he didn't want to be distracted by my screaming and thrashing...'

Omega let a silence fall between them. He removed a handheld medical scanner from an inner pocket of his coat and began to scan Zeta. Finally, looking at the scanner's display, he said: 'I need to see if I can repair some of the damage you sustained. There are buildings not far from here with computers and supplies that can help. I will not be gone long.'

Omega I, Zeta XVI, and whoever this Alpha android was, were created as part of a military programme that began life as The Adam Project.

The Adam Project, so named for the Creation myth of Adam and Eve, began in earnest nine hundred years prior. An expanding group of disenfranchised citizens who called themselves the Centurions, for their

Romanesque dedication to divide-and-conquer, were expanding their boundaries perilously close to space designated for the offices and palaces of the Empire. Skirmishes occurred along Imperial borders until it was decided that simple strength would not be enough to repel these malefactors.

It was then that the first children were adopted by the military; 'adopted', that was, against their parents' informed consent. Five and six years old's, covertly analysed for their potential receptivity to mechanical adaptation, then kidnapped, their parents told that they had died in an accident of some sort. Raised in sterility by a troop of wet nurses to comfort and a legion of scientists to study them, as they matured their bodies were merged with machines. Modifications brought them to an athletic and combative prowess unrivalled by anything that nature or discipline could have produced, while dulling that which records of the time refer to as 'the sensual faculties'.

Love, hate, sexual desire, and anything else unnecessary to the programming were sublimated. At the forefront of every new mind were the Orders, dictated by a select few handlers who decided the patterns of wars from fortified battlements towering high above their planets. Untroubled by fear or compassion these part human, part machine super-soldiers littered the wastelands of outer space with their enemies, reducing the Centurions to shadows.

Omega arrived at the edge of the city, just within view of the mountain inside which Zeta remained on his stony bunk. The only access points on all the buildings were garage doors large enough to accommodate tanks, the idea being that once you descended to the planet you climbed in a vehicle and were driven straight through; the military engineers who came here didn't come to spend time outside, soaking up the sun. Omega walked to the nearest building and its door.

Rather than risk wasting hours tinkering with its access panel, Omega used his hands to force a crease in the bottom of the door and, gaining purchase, lifted it up on its rollers. His modified hands barely registered the strain of a task that would have been impossible to even the strongest of 'natural' men. The room beyond was dim, though the opening door had triggered various computer terminals into life. Everything was connected and automated here, so the buildings resembled huge technological organisms.

The terminals displayed a crudely pixelated screensaver of Earth rotating on its axis. Omega plugged the scanner that he'd used on Zeta XVI into the nearest terminal's hard drive. The screensaver vanished and in its place appeared a dense list of analyses, diagnoses, and statistics that, once he had read their majority, told Omega that his new friend would soon be nothing more than dead flesh and spare parts.

In a large and expensive hotel by a bright blue sea, a young man in a white suit sat in a room washed with sunlight. His hair was chestnut brown and his eyes a brown so dark it was often mistaken for black, making his eyes look at first glance like snooker balls suspended in milk. Before him was a table laid with a single serving of cane sugar, a teabag, a cup and saucer, and a small flask of hot water. As he studied these objects he heard a knock on the door and, smiling to himself, asked the visitor in.

The man who entered wore a military suit, pea green, bedecked on the right breast with medals even though, as a merely administrative worker these days, the man in the white suit wondered how entitled he was to them. For the moment, however, he was diplomatic. 'Simon!' he cried, standing up and slapping his guest on the back while shaking his hand.

'Please, take my chair. You must have had a long journey from the capital. I wish I could have come out to meet you, but as I know you're aware, the bureaucrats and I don't exactly get along.'

'I doubt I could be any more aware of that, Peter' said Simon, allowing himself a slight smile. He was a thickly-built man, broad-shouldered and blonde, yet obviously thoughtful, and wary of the man he'd come to see. He was about to place the overstuffed manila folder he carried under his arm on the table, then noticed the tea things. Raising his eyebrows at Peter, he said 'for me or for you?'

'For both of us!' Peter replied, 'but they haven't yet sent up the second half of my order. It appears the kitchens are being monopolised by a troop of schoolgirls on a trip.' Peter took the tray with the tea things and laid it aside. They sat down and, leafing through his folder, Simon took out a stapled stack of papers. 'Peter Windbourne' he read, 'formerly designated Alpha VII.'

'Simon Harries, formerly designated Gamma V.' Simon smiled. Peter sensed the uneasiness behind it. 'Do you fear me, brother?'

'We are no longer brothers, Peter. Have you not yet come to understand that?'

Peter's smile was unwavering. 'The bonds

of family in the human world were, I thought, supposed to be sacred.'

Simon shifted in his seat and attempted a smile of levity equal to his companion's, though it was a challenge. Peter sensed that Simon was scared of him, which he supposed was natural enough; they hadn't seen each other in more than a hundred years, and their time together was characterised by violence that someone now living as a human, in human society, might wish to forget. But beyond that, Peter realised that Simon was also disgusted by him. He looked at Peter as one might look at a large insect with a bloody maw. In an even tone, Peter said, 'May I read your palm, old friend?'

'Excuse me?'

'In my attempt to live among human society I have been researching certain cultures. Once upon a time there were 'gypsies'; travelers who practiced 'magic' arts. One of these was the divination of personal destiny through the reading of lines on the palm of the hand.'

Simon smiled slightly. 'I'm aware' he said, 'my wife once dressed as a gypsy for Halloween.'

'Your wife!' replied Peter, 'I hadn't considered that you'd be married. Please, your palm? Humour me. Let me show you how much I've learned.' With clear reluctance Simon place his hand palm up on the table. Almost immediately he felt the muscles there freezing. He looked in shock at Peter, his eyes demanding an explanation. Peter's smile had now become a grin. 'Muscle-cripplers, attached to the underside of the table. I'm sure you recognise the technology, Gamma V. You would have used it several times to interrogate other android lifeforms. 'Interrogate', I'm assuming, is the word you'd prefer now that you consider yourself human again. 'Torture' is so ugly, so unyielding. So... robotic.'

Simon's other hand had balled into a fist and he now swung it at Peter, who darted quickly away to a standing position. 'What do you want from me?' said Simon, almost whispering in his shock and fear. Peter walked to the window. On a gently sloping rise of land two young children played with dolls; their parents sat on a picnic blanket in the shade of a nearby tree. Above, a small ship descended towards outer space; its size indicated that it carried tourists.

'Who was my mother?' Peter asked. He turned from the window and gazed at his prisoner. 'For that matter, Gamma V, who was yours? You have the pale complexion and auburn hair of a Scot. Are you Scottish? Was your mother named Agnes and did she read you Robert Burns as you lay in your crib?'

'You know I don't know who my mother was, or yours. No-one has that information anymore, not for hundreds of years. The records were destroyed once we reached maturity and were judged stable enough in our programming to enter the battlefield.'

'And you've never had any curiosity about what was in those records, not even now, not even when, wires or not, you're supposed to be a real live boy? Oh, brother, how I wish I was as dull and subservient as you.' Simon looked at the door to the hall. 'You said more tea was coming. Someone will be here.' Peter flicked his eyes at the tea tray as if just remembering it. 'I lied. I only ordered enough for one, and that one, brother, is you.'

Omega's ship hovered near the edge of the solar system as he sat listening to a radio transmission. Zeta had still been alive when he returned from the city with an armful of engineering odds and ends, more to prolong Zeta's life for a few more days than save it, which was impossible. Omega was impassive about death and, if it had been his own life guttering like a candle with no more wax to melt, he wouldn't have bothered taking anything.

He just would have sat down, cross-legged, and meditated until Death came. But just because a person is relatively unemotional doesn't mean that they don't understand the importance of emotions in others, or have a sense of duty. Zeta XVI, Omega knew instinctively from the way he spoke and his body language, had been living as a regular human for long enough that he shared their passions, their weaknesses.

He would want to feel that there was hope, that he wasn't going to die in a cave with only a strange, cold man for company. Omega gave him this as he went about attaching this bit of junk to that corrupted circuit, pretending without having to say anything that he was saving his life, that his core hadn't in fact been irreparably scorched by both an aggressive assault from a killing machine *and* a spaceship explosion. The killing machine was this weird, treacherous Alpha, who aroused Omega's mild curiosity the way a loose but painless toenail might aggravate someone else.

'Would it be okay if I slept... just for a while? I mean, that wouldn't hurt my chances would it?' Zeta had said at the end.

'That would be acceptable' said Omega, looking up from his work. Zeta smiled and sighed with relief. 'Thank you' he said, 'thank you, Omega. By the way, I don't know if this will mean anything to you, I mean if you care at all, but my human name, it's Jacob.'

'Sleep well, Jacob.'

The radio transmission sputtered and Omega made an adjustment to the equipment. Beyond the view screen of the main bridge was only blackness and stars. The transmission came through loud, and clear. '...from the capital of the Imperial Colony the murderer is presumed to have fled before the body could be found. Questions are being asked as to why the victim, a high-ranking administrative official in the Imperial War Office, wasn't kept under closer guard but was allowed to travel to a relatively unguarded recreational facility, alone, to interview a former android soldier believed by the War Office to potentially be a dangerous malefactor.'

The Imperial Colony, six months away if he could bring his ship up to light speed, was where Omega was headed. 'The documents that the victim, name as yet unrevealed to the media, brought to the interview are known to have contained profiles of various soldiers from the Super Soldier programme. The controversial programme, which ran secretly for more than half a millennium, has been slowly phased out as more preventative measures, including laser satellites, are implemented to protect against Imperial malefactors.

'It is believed that these measures were a motive in the killing as traditional warfare, 'the lifeblood of an active Super Soldier' according to one programme director, faces the threat of extinction. The victim's folder contained the profile of a Super Soldier named Omega I, who according to War Office records began a hermitage in the now abandoned Solum Et system six decades ago. Android soldiers were designated Omega for the extreme levels of violence they could both sustain and commit; as of this report an Imperial fleet is on its way to Solum Et to question this soldier, believed to be the last I class Omega still living.'

Omega silenced the radio receiver. His eyes were narrowed slightly as he processed what he had heard and tried to make a decision based on it. He recalled the gas planet in Solum Et, and the abandoned research stations many of which would still be hovering above it, not due to fall for at least another century.

It was said by the researchers that the energy radiated by the planet cleared your head and sharpened your intellect. He would go there to meditate and thereby decide his next move. It made as much sense to Omega as anything else that had happened recently, and that which would help him regain his treasured surety was welcome.

The stations that hovered above the gas planet looked like platforms in a video game. Alpha half expected a pixelated ape to start chucking barrels at him. He stood in the dome above one station, the shuttle he took from his ship to one side. He found an access panel on a stand, pressed a button, and descended the stairs revealed by a shifting floor tile.

Inside the station portable equipment lay in disarray, the computers frozen at various displays. It was as if the researchers fifty years ago had just dropped what they were doing and left, like a family dragged from their home midway through dinner. Dust soaked everything; even Alpha with his metallic fortified lungs paused briefly to cough.

The planet's atmosphere consisted of white and purple clouds in streaks like the trails left by aeroplanes, piled and twisted in frail ribbons. They seemed to be moving constantly, sometimes fading and sometimes coming into focus. When viewed you imagined that falling into the planet would be like falling into a ball of grape flavoured candyfloss.

Through a large display screen and across the gulf of the planet Alpha saw another station. Adjusting his eyes, that he had modified with technology stripped from the late Gamma V's, he was able to see through the opposite station's screen to where Omega sat cross-legged, eyes closed and meditating among the scientific detritus. Alpha gave himself a moment to enjoy the voyeurism.

'Poor little Indian' he said, 'the Pilgrim has come to repurpose your land.'

The thing that Alpha hadn't expected was that Omega's senses would be tuned to discern a stranger (the teleporter, as operated by Alpha, was silent). He had planned to approach his meditating victim like Hamlet sneaking up on uncle Claudius, dagger raised. He would then use the killing grip vastly improved by Zeta XVI's stolen hand to punch a hole through the back of Omega's neck, where a cluster of wires controlling the spine would be; only a hand of previously unknown strength could achieve this, and Alpha was up to the task.

Just as he reached the halfway point between the teleporter and Omega, however, the latter spun around, standing up, pulled a laser gun from his coat, and fired into Alpha's abdomen. Alpha was hurled against a computer terminal that buckled and dented beneath his weight, almost threatening to rip a hole in the station that would topple it into the gas. A little blood escaped the side of his mouth and, ignoring it, Alpha smiled, his smile seeming only slightly crazed at this point; he still felt in control.

'Why are you doing this?' said Omega.

'Haven't you ever wanted more, brother? Or are you as dull as all the others?' Omega thought. 'I can only repeat my question' he said, 'why are you doing this?'

Alpha laughed bitterly and stood up, with enough caution to not inspire his host to shoot again. 'I know that voice' he said, 'I fought alongside it for over a century. That was *my* voice, once upon a time. Cold and unemotional, without inflection, without even contractions in the language used. I'm two hundred years old and I've only been alive for the last fifty. How old are you, brother?'

'One hundred and eighty three.'

'Of course. I would have been seventeen, almost ready to spend my life fighting and killing for interests not my own, when your mother gave birth to you. You've never even wondered who she was, have you? Who your father was, whether they loved you, what your cultural heritage had been before the damned Imperial army snatched you and filled you with wires...'

'Wh-'

'Why am I doing this', right. Good question. 'You have some curiosity, at least.

Well, my brother, I'm not sure you'll understand as this involves individuality, not blind obedience to lesser beings, but here goes: I want to be a god.'

'Heck, I *am* a god, but one only growing as of now. I've yet to salvage enough scrap from my fellow Super Soldiers to be able, for instance, to travel space at light speed without a spaceship, or to fight off entire fleets, but I'll get there. One day I'll smash the Empire to rubble, and from that rubble build a *new* Empire where those still fully human will be the slaves of those now mechanical. You can fight me, but I'm merely the next step in our evolution, Omega, and I intend to be at the godhead of the new species.'

Omega fired again and the laser hit Alpha's abdomen, but this time the wounded area merely glowed as it healed itself, and Alpha remained standing upright, smiling ever broader. 'I'm adaptable, you see. Fire at me once, I fall. Fire at me twice, and not only has my body healed itself enough to recover, but it's adapted to the nature of the weapon and become immune to it.'

Omega considered this for only the time it took for Alpha to prepare a return attack, his fist raised and ready to destroy his brother's face. Omega stamped a hole through the floor of the station and the atmosphere outside rushed in, toppling it from its position so that it started to fall at great speed. After Zeta was dead he had used the body's remaining leg to improve his own two, gaining from the salvaged technology just enough strength to kick a hole in a spaceship (or, at least, a rather old and frail research station).

As the two soldiers plummeted towards the core of the planet, rolling around like marbles in a tin, an odd new emotion began to flower in Omega. He didn't know whether the station was strong enough to pass through the planet's core, and therefore whether he'd survive; Super Soldiers could breathe in space, but were they strong enough to storm the heart of a gas planet and come out on the other side? He noticed that he was nervous.

THE END?

LIFE CHANGES OF SUN

By Tapiwa MacHin

Tapiwa writes:
Life changes of sun is inspired by a lot of different western movies including international dramas, Asian to be precise. While planning and creating the story line, creating my characters was the best part of my story. I named them Sun and Jack (Sun is a Korean name can be spelled as Seon.) When I started my story line, I planned it out, but when I started writing the story, there were a lot of changes from the original I had drafted. I found my story had no ending. Then I remembered how I love stories with plot twists, so I had to create another story in the middle of a story and the ending turned out to be a little cliff hanger.

I

Sun went to the coffee shop for her lunch break. It was crowded and she could smell, almost taste the coffee. She left her coat on the seat and followed the growing line, her hunger for a Latte growing by the second. When it arrived it looked perfect: creamy and rich. She added extra sugar, needing the energy boost. That was when the man beside her at the counter turned to make his order, and knocked the cup from her hand. Furious, she looked down at her dress, then up at him. Her fury vanished in an instant when she saw his face, replaced by the thought, 'oh... he's GORGEOUS.' Remembering that he had spilled her perfect latte and ruined her dress, the anger came back and she purposely trod on his foot as he tried to apologise, a little aggressive act that came instinctively to her.

Back at the office Sun spoke to her secretary, May, who was also her best friend, about her schedule for that week. May saw the giant stain down the front of Sun's dress but said nothing, assuming that Sun had had one of her clumsy moments at lunch. Clumsiness was one of her weaknesses. Sun, however, saw May looking and, rolling her eyes, explained about the man in line. 'And the worst part' she concluded, 'was that he didn't even say sorry!' Inwardly she told herself off for leaving out that he tried to apologise but she trod on his foot before he could. Still, she felt justified in her fury. Damnit, he'd ruined her lunch break! Her eyes full of anger, she listened as May changed the subject: 'I almost forgot, you've got that meeting with those potential investors tomorrow!' Sun smiled. Finally, some good news...

'Meeting scheduled here, at her offices,' May replied.

II

The morning of the meeting Sun woke up earlier and dressed more carefully than usual. She arrived at work earlier than her secretary just to sort out some paperwork for a client who was due to have surgery in the following weeks. Or, at least, said paperwork was her excuse for coming in early. May arrived an hour later to find Sun already in her office. 'What a surprise!' said May, 'I'm in shock. What's going on, Sun? You are never in this early no matter what meetings you've got to attend.'

Sun looked up from her desk and replied, 'Don't act so surprised. I need my best friend right now. I'm anxious about this meeting... What if no one wants to invest in us, or the investor turns out to be a con artist like last time? I just have so many worries about the business, you know, and I've already used up some of my savings to keep us on our feet. We could end up being jobless, even homeless. Can you blame me for being here early?' May looked at Sun and said, 'I can see you barely slept last night. But I need you to calm down. You over-think things, and you're getting yourself worked up. Life is all about taking risks, and anyway, this time I did the background.

'I've done checks on all the investors, Sun, before setting up this meeting. I have your back, so don't worry so much.' May went back to the front desk just in case there were any clients waiting. One of the investors, Mr. Jack Sullivan, walked in and spoke to May, who directed him to the waiting area. May couldn't help but admire the hunk that he was. He was like a giant teddy bear, his scent pervading every room he passed through and object he touched; that's how amazing he was. After a few minutes May gave Sun a call to remind her that it was almost time for the meeting. Before she even got the chance to pass by May's desk, however, Sun had been informed via texts that all the investors but one had cancelled on her. She told May this, and was pleased to be told in return that the remaining investor was in the waiting area, and according to May he was 'scrumptious.' Sun smiled and said, 'That's what you said about the con artist.'

'I know, but still...' May replied, 'it's too bad I'm married with a baby on the way...'

III

Sun opened the door, wondering if May's erotic rapture was a joke. She had to remind herself to stay calm and professional, however, as when she saw the remaining investor she couldn't believe her eyes. It was him! The bastard from the coffee shop! Judging by the deer-in-headlights expression in his own eyes, he too was startled.

None the less, they were both businesspeople. The meeting proceeded as planned with Sullivan agreeing to partner with Sun and invest in her company, which dealt in plastic-surgery supplies. Personal issues were put on hold while they were discussing business; representatives for both parties were even called in before the signing of the contract to make sure everything was legal and by the book. After the contract was signed and everything was official, the lawyers left and Sullivan and Sun stayed behind to 'talk business.'

It was nothing they hadn't discussed before, but they felt that they needed to go over it again. Phone numbers were exchanged and Mr. Sullivan asked Sun to go out for a meal, or drinks, since they had just become partners. Since Sun had been holding it in throughout the meeting, it finally came bursting out of her when she said,

'You're not going to spill a drink on my dress again, are you?' A little shocked at the sudden surfacing of that incident, he protested that he had looked for her, even asked some of the people in the shop if they knew where she worked, because he was trying to apologise and pay for the dry cleaning. He said that he didn't really get a good look at her face, and that was why he looked surprised when she mentioned the incident.

'At any rate' he concluded with a cheeky smile, 'my expensive shoes were ruined and I have a swollen foot!'

She let herself smile back and replied, 'Dinner at seven. Pick me up at this address.' She jotted on her pad, tore out the page, and gave it to him. 'Don't be late, time is money.' Mr. Sullivan fixed his tie as he left the room, just behind her.

IV
May was busy as Sun walked past her desk, and didn't notice her. Sun had planned this to her advantage, not wanting to be assaulted by

the inevitable stream of questions May would have for her. She'd want to know all that had happened with Mr. Sullivan, all the details.

Later that day, however, May noticed Sun had left work early and remarked to herself that Sun was normally the last one to leave the office. Putting her nosy shoes on, she texted Sun, *'It's unusual for you to be out before me'*, to which Sun curtly replied, *'Am having PROFESSIONAL dinner with new BUSINESS partner.'*

Sun knew that May would have a cheeky smile on her face, when she sent the last text. Sun explained in an unprompted follow-up text, sure that May would eventually wring the information from her anyway, that Mr. Sullivan had been the man who'd spilt her coffee down her dress. Intrigued, May replied, *'You didn't mention how YUMMY he was when you told me about that.'* Sun was sitting on her couch in a dressing gown, towel around her head, having just stepped out of the shower. She smiled at her phone.

'Well...' she wrote back, *'It didn't seem important. My dress was a mess!'*

May, sat behind her desk and laughing at her phone, replied, *'But you did notice...'*

'You know me,' wrote Sun, *'don't mix business and pleasure.'*

'*Sun! When was the last time you were in a relationship?!*'

Sun took her meaning. '*I know, I know*' she protested, '*not since university. But he doesn't seem that in to me.*'

'*Want to call?*'

'*What if someone comes into the office? They won't think we're very professional if they see the secretary gossiping on the phone.*'

'*You over-think things, just like with this guy. But I guess you SHOULD hurry up and get ready for your date.*'

'*IT'S NOT A DATE.*' Sun tossed her phone aside.

Mr. Sullivan, *Jack*, arrived on time to pick her up.

'So where are we going?' she asked.

'A friend gave me a recommendation,' he said. They arrived at a posh, well-organised restaurant with waiters and waitresses who were excellent hosts. Enjoying their dinner and drinks, they forgot the incident at the coffee shop and started talking like old friends. The spark between them blossomed like a firework. Or maybe it was a shooting star...

After dinner he took her home, and from then on he started taking her to dinner in secret, not even May knew about their private liaisons. When he returned from his business in some foreign country, the first thing he would do was call on Sun. They were growing on each other, and perhaps not even really noticing it. Sun would certainly have never acknowledged to herself that she missed him when he was away.

Months passed by and in the end, of course, they were forced to admit their liaisons, if only by their own desire to share their happiness. If May wasn't happy with being left out of the loop, she was at least happy that her friend wasn't married to her job anymore.

V

A year later, with news of a baby on the way, Jack began planning a surprise engagement party for himself and Sun. Sun was four months pregnant and aware that May would be throwing a baby shower for her; what she hadn't been told was that the shower would end in a proposal, and thereafter become an engagement party.

The celebration was planned down to the last detail. Friends and family were invited, but it was Sun's tradition that a baby shower should be a 'girls only' affair. Knowing that the baby would be a girl, because Sun and Jack had chosen to be told the gender, the guests brought pink gifts and showered the mother-to-be with pink roses. The hotel chosen for the event was impeccably modest in a posh, stylish way. The dress code was adhered to and everyone showed up looking fashionable. 'It's just more me' Sun had said when deciding on the dress code.

As the night wore on the girls only rule was relaxed and men began to arrive. Jack was driving down when he received a phone call. He pulled into a layby to take it, and heard an unknown voice say, 'You have been compromised. You need to take your family and lie low.' Before he could answer, the call had been ended. Confused and starting to get scared he didn't even feel the impact of the van that hit his car, shoving it towards the side of a bridge through which it was likely to fall and crash into the canal below.

He came to his senses just in time to slam the brakes on, but the driver's side of the car was badly damaged, and when he tried to open the door the last thing he saw was Sun's missed calls listed on his phone.

Sun kept calling but not getting through until she assumed that his phone had been turned off. At that moment what seemed like hundreds of men in black riot-gear, holding weapons, burst into the hotel and dragged Sun away from the party to some waiting cars outside. The room was chaotic, and Sun kept asking in her panic what it was that she had done, why was she being arrested.

One of the men explained that he was a secret agent, she hadn't done anything wrong, and all would be explained once they reached their destination. Sun's heart was pounding so hard that everyone could hear it, until at last they realised her pregnant condition and tried to comfort her.

They arrived at a nondescript house in the middle of nowhere. Someone explained to Sun that it was a witness protection house, and for her to be protected she would have to leave her company in the hands of someone she trusted (May, she thought) and not have any more contact with anyone she knew for the foreseeable future. She was told that Jack had been on his way to propose to her when a fatal accident occurred that the police were still investigating. 'But why am I here?!' she cried in her confusion and despair, 'Why is my life in danger? What's happening?' Tears rolled down her face as she tried to come to terms with the loss of her husband.

A man walked in and everyone else left the room. He sat down beside her and, revealing himself to be a secret agent, explained everything to her, from the beginning:

Jack was an agent himself and had moved

to the area around where Sun lived and worked as part of an undercover operation. The day he bumped into and spilt her coffee over her was no coincidence. Jack had been following her, studying her routine, thinking it through. The incident in the coffee shop was the result of him trying to introduce himself to her and gain her phone number. But things didn't go as planned. So instead he posed as an investor in order to get close to her.

'I won't go into too much detail about the mission' said the agent, 'because much of it is still highly classified, but he was meant to disappear after a month or so, leaving you a large amount of money through the investments he made to your company. However, by then he was starting to develop serious feelings for you. He was in love with you, Sun, for real, but he was also in too deep with the mission, and now it seems that his enemies have caught up with him. I know this is a hell of a lot to take in, especially so suddenly and in your condition, but we really had no other choice than to bring you here, as the people who killed your fiancée might now be after you. They might think you know something, and we couldn't take that risk.'

Beyond the confusion, Sun was devastated. She didn't even know if she had time or energy to grieve, and cry. The future spread itself out before her as an endless churning mass. 'Who were you, Mr. Sullivan?' she asked silently...

THE FATE OF A SOUL

By C.R. Mallett

His eyes were like no other... Those eyes shining so bright, as though the sun was reflecting on a pair of rubies.

It all began on the 21st June 1984.

That's when the darkness first took over my life; you see, I lost my husband from a robbery that had gone wrong...

I blame myself for what had happened; if only I had never taken that first drag of a cigarette; maybe then he would still be here to keep me safe from all this madness, because I feel trapped... broken... scared.

Please someone... Please save me from this monster that haunts me; this red eyed man who lingers in the darkest corners of a room wearing nothing but lost shadowed souls beneath his long leather jacket.

I can feel him, every time I close my eyes. It's as though he is following me... Why?

I saw him last night in my dreams. I was sitting on a stool, in the middle of a big dark room. He was there too; I could feel him breathing down the back of my neck, smelling my fear. I think that is what was making him stronger.

His eyes were burning my skin; he slowly pulled his hands out of his leather jacket, and flew towards me, grabbing my arm tightly before the floor went beneath me.

'HELP ME,' I cried. I'm falling into something that seems to be a bottomless pit. I cover my eyes from the bright lights that are before me, getting closer and closer...

Then I woke up.

My heart was racing. Sweat was pouring off my body and I needed to go into the bathroom to refresh myself. As I dipped my face into the sink and splashed water over me, I looked up and moved my hands...

The reflection in the mirror showed that my arm had a handprint pressed into it.

It was from him. But I thought it was a dream? But it's real. How do I stop this?

I drink a lot of caffeine, just so I don't sleep. I'm scared and sleep now is torturing my soul.

I tried to tell my Psychiatrist about what was going on. I told him about the handprint; I even showed him the evidence, but he didn't believe me.

Do you know what he said?

'Donna, if you see a doctor they can help you get over this.' He preached at me like it was my fault!

'WHAT?' I answered viciously. 'You can't seriously think I did this to myself? I would never do that! Why would I do that?'

As I looked into his eyes with a dark glare, I could tell exactly what he was thinking,

'Excuse me Donna, I just need to take this. I will be with you again shortly,' said Dr. Mason, answering his phone.

Why is he acting as though I have committed some sort of crime? I'm no criminal. I'm the victim, I thought to myself. Maybe I should just leave.

As I got up and walked towards the door two men wearing white clothing came through. I got worried so turned back only to be stopped by Dr. Mason.

'I've made arrangements for you to spend some time at the mental health hospital Donna. I promise they will take good care of you.' He whispered.

I didn't want to go. 'No please, you can't do this! it wasn't me!' I cried desperately, but he wasn't listening to my cries for help. He looked at me like I was crazy.

The two men grabbed my arms and dragged me out of the building throwing me into a stuffy hot van. I felt like I couldn't breathe.

When I arrived we were greeted by a priest. 'Oh Father, please help me,' I begged him, but he didn't want to know either.

They took me into a small room with nothing but a bed with ties. A few more men came in to help them restrain me because I was fighting so hard. I was terrified.

They strapped me down until I could barely move. One of the nurses came in with a tray full of needles and liquids.

'What is that stuff?' I asked them.

'This here is some medicine. It will help you get some sleep,' the nurse replied..

'No please. I don't want to sleep! He's going to hurt me again. He is coming for me,' I begged.

They continued to prepare me for the injection whilst four other nurses held my arms so I didn't move. They all ignored my pleading cries for help. As the nurse came towards me with the needle and injected the fluid into my arm she told me,

'There is nothing to fear but fear itself.'

Then I fell asleep.....

RED SCARE

By Joe Ryan

Joe writes:

Red scare is the first story I have tried writing. I have found over the years that I had been trying to tell myself stories in my head but have never done so until now.

Doing this project has given me a new respect to those who write not just books on a regular basis but to all of those who make creative material, whether that be a film or a video game.

The initial idea came during my course lessons; I've been fascinated by the Soviet Union and its ideals for many years and the ideas formed from there. Actually developing the story caused many days of creative block before I finally stumbled upon an idea that would take it beyond the concept of simply being a version of The Americans, *reversed to be set in the Soviet Union, and this concept will eventually drive the story forward towards it conclusion.*

The relief of having a concept that could be unique was an indescribable relief and ultimately, I feel will make the world my protagonist lives in, very groovy in a weird sort of way.

Finding time to be able to write the story can actually be quite hard, no matter how much you like the concept and even then, you can be assured that you will think your work is an unbelievably awful story that belongs on the shelves with Atlas Shrugged. *(See XKCD's Bookshelf comic strip). I personally find that late at night, when all is calm, is a perfect time to let creativity flow; don't be saddened if you can't churn out many pages a night as taking scenes from your head and transcribing them is a draining process. Some nights you may get 500 words, some nights you will struggle to get more than 50. What is important is that you keep working on it.*

To be able to get something down onto paper after so many years is oddly empowering. I have found, even if I never get this published or read by another soul I would have created a world that is entirely my own and that no one else can touch. The segment is only a sample of what I have written so far, and I look forward to writing and developing the story further as time goes on.

Chapter 1

A commanding officer of MI6 sat at her desk in her office overlooking the river in London. This morning she was briefing a new recruit into the service, which was always a nerve-wracking experience.

Her gut feeling regarding them was all too reliable, built over years of experience of being an intelligence officer herself. Their files may often show their great personal qualities for the job, but no matter how much people said otherwise, she could not be convinced that any amount of training could prepare them for the challenges of their work.

It was 1979 and mistakes could not be made at any cost, not with the Cold War raging. The consequences of it were too high for her to imagine. Time always dragged before a new recruit was due in; it was the moment of truth for her and the service and there was no turning back.

At quarter past nine the door cautiously opened, a young, tall women walked through, wearing a blue overcoat. She looked little over twenty.

There was a brief unbroken spell of silence with only the clock ticking. There were nerves on both sides. The commanding officer broke the silence in an unexpectedly soft tone, in Russian that was gained from her years in the field. She wanted to be sure that this person was up to the assignment she was about to give her.

'Kate?'

'Yes,' she replied back in the same language, her accent still had a slight overtone of where she came from, but was too subtle to not cause suspicion.

The commander looked at her files, her photo was a spot on match and her signature was verified also. She then began to open her log of the operation and started to brief Kate, continuing in Russian.

'New recruits often get simple missions; a few months in an obscure location collecting information gathered from public sources, more like a holiday if I'm honest. You're skipping that phase and heading straight into the cold war. We're sending you to Moscow.'

Kate felt honoured that she had been trusted with such a task, but then felt her heart about to rip clean out of her chest. She had been sent immediately into the lion's den and one false move could bring her crashing down.

'Why me?' Kate asked. 'There must be many more people in this very building with experience I don't have, years of it as matter of fact and yet here I am chosen over them?'

The commander swiftly responded, 'That is certainly true; indeed there are many, but it would be foolish to consider that this building isn't being monitored for people coming in and people going out. All experienced Intelligence Officers do eventually pick up records, and the likelihood is that the Soviet Intelligence Services already know about them.'

'So you need a clean slate to go in, one completely off the record? Is that because of the sensitivity of what we are going to be doing?' asked Kate.

'Completely correct,' the Commander replied. 'We've used the stickiest criteria for this mission possible, and you have come out on top. Make no mistake, this mission will require patience and a great deal of resourcefulness, but we strongly believe you are the person for this job. You will receive further details when you arrive in Moscow.'

And with that the briefing was over and they shook hands.

It all seemed a blur to Kate, as she was led away from the Commanders office, down the steps into the back of the building, a car waiting to drive her swiftly away. She arrived at the airport and departed soon after. Passing through security, oddly using her British passport, she was met in Moscow by the driver in the lounge, and given Soviet documentation, and a key. She arrived at her apartment in the dead of night....

GENRE AND CHARACTERISATION

T. Kitching writes:

There are lots of different genres that you can write your story for. From the young to the old, most readers have a favourite style that they like to read or hear being read. Your story can be easy to follow to let the reader just get swept away or you can get the reader to really think and get involved, but most importantly I think, is to have the reader experience the emotions that you yourself felt when you wrote it.

We were tasked with thinking of different genres: Crime, Science Fiction, Horror, Romance, Fantasy, Ghosts, Mysteries, Fairy Tale, Children's, Young Adults, Adult Fiction, Non Fiction

We were then asked to think up a Character; their world and the genre that we would like to use. I tried to break my character down into the following categories:-

Name, Age, Gender, Description, Personality, Year, Country, (Planet if Sci-Fi).

I came up with the following:-
Josie Reah, 30's, Female, English, Tall, Medium build, Dark hair, Hazel eyes, Dresses smart. She is smart, confident, knowledgeable, and knows what she wants. She has a good memory.

I decided on the genre: Romantic /Horror / Mystery, set in the 2000's, in England.

I then came up with a bit of background for the character: -

Her long term relationship has ended. Her father is alive, but her mother has passed. She is an only child; bullied in the past and now suffers from depression. She is moving to a new flat with her cat, and has a new job as a Teaching Assistant

I started to think about the story:-
Starting her new job, she gets a huge crush on the head teacher but she's not sure on taking another chance on love. They get

thrown together when teachers start to get murdered in gruesome ways and they try to solve the mystery of why and who?

Whilst I was thinking more about my story another popped into my head and I felt that the new story was more feasible for me to write so I decided to continue with that.

Name. Josie Reah. Age. 18, Female. Red head, average build. Funny, kind and loving.

Genre. Ghost/Supernatural, Young adult set in the 2000's in Dovercourt, Essex. Her family consists of Mum, Dad and much younger twin brother and sister and a Pet Cat.

This is the story I chose to write:
A young girl discovers she's died; tries to connect with her family to find out what happened. I was going to write this story as a murder mystery at first but as I discovered whilst writing, it began to take on a life of its own and the story played more to my strengths and knowledge.

THE DEATH OF JOSIE RHEA

By T. Kitching

DEATH

There was nothing noticeable about the day I
died except, I DIED!

Such pain, the aching and muscle spasms;
my head felt heavy as if the clouds were
building, but could I see the light!.

'What just happened? What am I doing
down here?' I forced myself to open my eyes
and as the darkness cleared I could see sky
through unfocused fauna and flora. I felt the
cold on my back as I lay there, had it been
raining I couldn't really remember but I felt
wet. I managed to move my hand across my
body, my muscles were now starting to ease
their vice-like grip. My body was dry yet my
head felt wet and sticky. Blood!, oh my God
there was blood, on my hand; from my head.
Then I heard the train... 'This train is for

Harwich Town only.' I could hear the faint patter of feet boarding and alighting the train as the doors opened... PING! PING! PING! then the train pulled away.

The Hangings, that's it. I was in the Hangings. I'd gone for a walk, it was a lovely day after all. Yet...How did I end up down here? I got slowly to my feet, feeling a bit unsteady I attempted to brush myself down. Clumsy Cow I thought; you must have fallen over. I turned towards home...THUD! I wasn't steady enough yet, I must have hit my head a little too hard. Laying there I turned my head towards the sea breeze, only to be met by my own face peering between foliage, lifeless beside me.

The vice like grip now clung to my chest as a whelk does to the sea defenses at low tide. I scrambled backwards on my hands and knees, 'I can't breathe! I can't breathe!' I struggled to repeat, whilst trying to cough my still lungs into life. Slowly placing two fingers shakingly to my neck, it was confirmed, I had no pulse; I was dead and all alone with my own corpse.

I sat there for an eternity trying to come to grips with my own mortality. 'This can't be!' I finally screamed. 'It's all a dream, wake up...wake up!' I pounded my fists either side of my head as I sat there with my head on my knees.

Nope, it's still there, just lying there, motionless. I wasn't brave enough to look fully; I was a child again peeking through my fingers when playing hide and seek. Maybe I should try counting to 10, and then this may all go away.

'...8...9...10, here I come ready or not!' It was still there nothing had changed. I began to cry but no tears came. Maybe, I thought; that's because ghosts can't cry!

FAMILY

'Mum, oh God Mum! She'll kill me when I don't come home' I paused for a second taking in my last statement.

I got to my feet and scrambled up the steep uneven hill to the path, only reaching the top by getting on to my hands and knees. The Hangings was a woodland short cut between Parkeston Village and Dovercourt. It was called the Hangings because large trees either side would hang over you in places like archways and not because, as I was told when I was a child, that people used to be hanged there.

Oh! I suppose now it will be known locally as the place that that girl was found dead. I surprised myself at how flippant I was dead. I realised I could feel no physical pain; I was walking on marshmallows instead of the solid tarmac pathway beneath my feet. Sound, smell and colour; everything was becoming stronger and more vibrant compared to the now muted world I had known.

I would say I felt my heart pounding from nervousness as I got to my street, but really it wasn't.

I had passed no one on the way; they would have shrieked. I'm sure they would have, as all I could see of my reflection in car windows was a whitewashed version of myself; just the faint colour of my purple top, blue jeans and my now bloody and matted red hair.

I stood at my front door... do I knock?

I waited as if it would open of its own free will. Silly that all that was between me and my home was this unassuming door, yet it felt impenetrable to me now. 'Shit! Why doesn't death come with a hand book?' I said to myself, why has no one come to guide me? Grandad! Aunt Joan! At this moment I'd settle for Great Uncle Tom and I couldn't stand him, any more than I could stand Marmite.

I could hear movement coming from inside the house.

'Riley!, Minah!' Mum shouted; a lump came into my throat. Mums voice sounded so perfect to my ears resembling beautifully chimed bells. I could then hear in response the twins coming down the stairs, not in their usual childish way but slow and steady as if counting each tread and rise with their tiny feet.

I'll never get to give them their presents I got them for their birthday, I thought. I won't see their excited faces as they run down stairs trying not to fall over one another to get to the post on the mat; which will, on that day be mainly cards. Screaming, 'that's for me, that one's mine!' between themselves as they sort them into piles. Mum would then sit them down in the front room, whilst Dad slowly made his way down stairs still half asleep. Cards would be discarded quickly when no money was involved, and Mum would be demanding who the cards are from trying to make a mental note of who to thank. The excitement will climax at the opening of Nana and Grandpa's cards, because there'll be an Argos voucher in each, normally £50 to which they have already picked out their gifts from the rather dog eared pages of the catalogue. The presents will come next. The presents!

GRIEF

The Teddies are under my bed in a green bag, hidden from prying eyes. I didn't tell Mum or Dad that I'd bought them, let alone where they were; I hadn't even wrapped them yet...I thought I had time!

My thoughts were broken by the sound of a car pulling up to a halt. The men sitting in the car looked as if they were from the movie Men in Black and the car too.

Click! The impenetrable door opened.

'Dad!' I reached towards him instinctively, in that blissful moment I had forgotten I was dead; then I proceeded to stumble right through him. I could feel his love, as we passed through each other; in one beat of his heart. I regained my balance. Mum and the twins were in the hallway, Mum was adjusting Riley's tie then Minah's head band. Mum had on her favourite Lilac dress and the twins were wearing their navy and white outfits. Bugger! Were we supposed to be going somewhere?, Hang on!, I thought... Are they really going without me, don't they care where I am and that I'm not back yet! I turned to Dad who was now talking to one of the men and shaking his hand; Dad had his suit on.

'What!' I said aloud, 'what the...' I turned to look at Mum.

'In there, go and get them,' she said as she ushered the twins into the front room. Looking back at Dad, his gaze was attentively fixed on another black car, slowly making its way along the street.

'No! Oh God, No!' I screamed, my heart

158

was now in my mouth, beating or not. Mum stepped out of our home, followed slowly by Riley and Minah with tears in their eyes and now the twins were hugging a fluffy teddy each in their little arms; the teddies for their birthday! At the road side Mum burst into tears at the sight of the second car that had now pulled up, and Dad comforted her and the twins with his embrace. I read the letters through the car window, white and purple against dark mahogany. J..O..S..I..E.

I took several dragged steps backwards until my body collided with our bay window; trying desperately to take in the events unravelling before my eyes.

'Mum, Dad!' I shouted, 'I'm here, for God's sake look at me; listen to me...PLEASE'!

Running towards them all, I was now waving my arms frantically trying to get their attention; whilst they stood in their comforting embrace.

'I'm here, that can't be me; I only left the house this morning; God I've only just left my body behind in the Hangings!' I fell to my knees at the roadside, my shouts and gestures were to no avail; not a glance or murmur in acknowledgment to my grief at the realisation that this was indeed my funeral.

'They have no idea I'm here!'.

How much time has actually passed; 1 week...2...3... Looking towards my family in their huddle I noticed a bright colour out of the corner of my eye; it was the Daffodils in the garden which were in full bloom, yet they hadn't been when I last left the house. I rose to my feet not sure of what I was going to do. 'Is this it!' I exclaimed. 'Am I supposed to wonder un-noticed, un-heard? What's the point!'.

I felt lost and alone; so alone. I had nowhere and no one to turn to, for the first time in my life, and it wasn't even my life; it was my death. My family broke apart and the twins followed by Mum and then Dad slowly climbed into the car, the man in black closed the door then walked to the front of the vehicle. Facing the car he nodded then turned and steadily walked a short distance down the street followed by the car carrying my family and preceding that was the vehicle carrying the Mahogany coffin with my body in it. I stood there helpless as the man in black got into the car and I watched the procession slowly advance around the corner and out of sight.

ALONE
That moment of realisation. The wanting and the longing will do no good, yet you still hope.

I slowly walked the few steps back to my

home, turned, and with my back against the door, slid down onto the cold worn door step; putting my hands on my knees and resting my head back against the hard glass. The clouds in the sky were few yet I watched them change their way across the perfect blue. The smell of the daffodils was now eclipsed by the smell of the Chinese restaurant coming to life further down the street. People passed; some glancing briefly at our house as if saying a silent prayer in acknowledgement, others unknowing to the sorrow that had befallen our little terraced house. I could hear traffic from the town, and in the distance, I could make out the noises from Cliff Park; birds were chirping and children were giggling; the sounds were rising in the heat of the day.

'The world goes on its merry way I see!'

For a while I just felt numb, insignificant; dead. I started to contemplate what might be going on at my funeral, who might have turned up to pay their last respects, what may have been said about me; including the obvious... She was eighteen, so young and gone too soon. I rested my head on my knees at this point feeling so very sorry for myself.

Meow!

I raised my head to see Dewy, our cat sat in front of my feet staring...

'You looking at me, Can you... see me?!'
Dewy sat and meowed again this time tilting his
head to the side to receive the stroke from my
outstretched hand.

'I can feel you Dewy!' I exclaimed. Dewy
purred as if responding to my own excitement.

'I don't know how, but I can feel you
Dewy; you wonderful cat you.' I resisted the
urge to pick him up and kiss him; people would
be surprised to see a big furry ginger tabby
floating in midair. 'I'll wait until they come
home, when they see you flying Dewy; they will
know I'm here'

Dewy sat and washed himself seemingly
indifferent to the fact I was technically a ghost,
he rolled onto his back as he always did; ready
to receive the belly rub that the position
demanded.

HOPE
Eyes are the windows to the soul... the all
Seeing Eye... the lenses for recording
memories. I think I dozed off if that's possible,
whilst awaiting their return from my funeral.

'Darn!' I exclaimed scanning the garden
for Dewy.

'Dewy where have you gone?' A slight panic
started to creep in. I got to my feet calling his
name repeatedly; 'Dewy, Dewy! Puss...puss!'

between calling him I clicked my tongue against my teeth trying to get him to hear me. I heard a faint meow from the other end of the street. I could then see Dewy doing his parkour between the posts and running effortlessly balanced along the walls of the front gardens to get to me.

'There you are!' He gave a short high pitched purr in reply as he came to a halt, then sat on our post curling his tail around his feet. As I gave him a fuss I could tell that the day was coming to a close, as the last rays of the sun struggled to cast its shadow. A taxi pulled up; they were back.

I actually held my nonexistent breath as they all got out of the taxi and made their way to the front door. I nearly picked up Dewy and thrust him in front of them there and then but seeing their faces I stopped myself. Maybe right now wasn't the time to let them know I was here. They filed through the doorway; Riley and Minah followed by Mum who had opened the door and turned the light on; then lastly my Dad with his hand reassuringly resting on Mums shoulder. Dad turned in the doorway and smiled at me.

'Come on,' he said motioning with his hand to come in. I took a step forward smiling.

'Dad!'

'Where have you been all day Dewy?' jumping down from the post Dewy made his way to the front door then stopped, turned and walked a short distance away. Although I felt heartbroken that it was the cat that Dad was actually talking to and not me, I seized the moment and made my way indoors when Dad stepped from the door way to pick Dewy up.

'I've got Dewy,' Dad said as he shut the door behind us then he gently dropped Dewy to the floor. I made my way up the stairs opposite and watched through the spindles as Dad went past into the kitchen to join the others. I could hear the kettle being put on.

'Tea?' Mum asked.

'Mmm,' Dad replied. Dewy had come up the stairs to me then proceeded to wash behind his ears with his paw as we both sat there.

'Oh! Dewy,' I said softly reaching my hand towards him for comfort. As I touched his soft fur I felt a tingling in my fingertips, which surged up my arm and my vision went blurry. I couldn't move my hand away. I blinked repeatedly trying to focus. My sight returned but it wasn't mine. It was Dewy's eyes I was looking through and it was no longer evening. The lights were off and the hallway was gently illuminated by the sun shine coming through the glass paneled front door.

Knock… Knock, Mum walked past the stairs to the front door; on opening it Riley and Minah walked in.

'Where's Josie?' asked Mum as they took their shoes off in the hallway.

'She not here?' Riley replied.

'Yeah, that's why I'm asking,' Mum joked whilst closing the door. Minah smirked whilst heading into the kitchen stating, 'we stayed in the Hangings to look for tadpoles; maybe she went to Lin's?'

'Ok, but you know you should all stay together,' said Mum picking up their shoes.

'Make sure you wash your hands please,' she demanded while prompting Riley into the kitchen before her; messing up his hair with her spare hand.

I was released from the vision as Dewy broke away to go down stairs; having been called for his dinner.

That's right; we'd been for a walk through the Hangings… together! I didn't want to hang around so left them looking for tadpoles; I was making my way home, and I tripped!

I started to feel sick. 'Oh God seriously, I'm dead because I was unable to put one foot in front of the other!' I shook my head slowly in disbelief at my own clumsiness, and the pain it had caused.

KNOWING

Knowledge is not always a good thing!

I positioned myself on the door mat at the front door to get a better look into the kitchen yet wanting to distance myself from the pain I had caused; part of me was wishing that someone would open the door so I could escape but with the clock chiming 10 o'clock I knew the likelihood was zero.

'Off to bed now you two,' I heard Mum say. '*Good night and I love you,*' was said by all with each kiss and cuddle. I watched the twins make their way slowly up the stairs.

'Good night; I love you too,' I said as I had done hundreds of times before but this time there was no reply. I could see Mum beginning to cry.

'I miss her so much,' she said through the tears and sobs.

'I know, I miss her too.' Dad answered his voice breaking off at the end into sobs of his own. Mum and Dad embraced trying to give each other strength, Dad with his arm still tightly around Mum, walked her to the bottom of the stairs.

'You go up love,' he urged. 'I'm just going to turn the lights off.' Mum made her way up stairs blowing her nose into a piece of tissue given to her by Dad from his pocket. Dad turned off the kitchen light after making sure the back door was locked then making his way to the stairs he called, 'Night Dewy,' before ascending. Dewy swaggered his way towards me then head butted my legs as he brushed his body against me wanting affection. I scooped him up in my arms pulling him to my chest and rubbed my head next to his. I needed comfort.

Again the tingling started, and then I was seeing through Dewy's eyes once more; I could see Mum and Dad sitting at the kitchen table Mum cried 'NO!' her shoulders shaking as she began to sob. Dad lowered his head and covered his eyes with one hand as the other reached for my Mum's. I then heard a woman's voice say,

'I'm very sorry for your loss, please if you need anything you can contact us on this number.' Chairs moved and my Dad rose from his seat and escorted out two police officers. The Police Woman patted me on the head as she went by. Then I was running from the front door through to the kitchen and jumping up onto the counter; Dewy's speed and agility I could now feel for myself. Dad shut the door after the police officers left and returned to Mum, who was now standing by the sink. They hugged each other so tightly, crying into each other's shoulders; I wished Dewy would turn his head away at this point but I was forced to watch.

YOU HEARD IT HERE

Why do we cry when really it does no good? You can't breathe properly, or see, and you always look awful afterwards.

'I'd better phone Mum,' Mum said breaking away from Dad. 'I want the kids home.'

'OK love,' answered Dad wiping his teary eyes on the sleeve of his shirt. 'Do you want me to...'

'No!' interrupted Mum making her way around the table to the phone hanging on the wall above me. Mum shooed me out of the way, I was heading up the stairs at speed; now I could only hear a one way conversation.

'Mum...she's dead!' she mustered before it went quiet; then Mum was crying inconsolably. Dad must have taken the phone from Mum, as all I heard next was his quivering voice trying to hold back tears.

'We'll tell them, when you drop them off. Bye May.' We didn't have to wait long for them to arrive.

With my view from the stairs I could tell the twins knew already that it wasn't good news. I could tell by their faces as Nana brought them through the door: it was at this point Nana too fell apart. The twins ran to Mum's outstretched arms, they all hugged each other holding on as tightly as they could. Nana hugged Dad before making her way to Mum and the twins.

'I'm so sorry,' she said, glancing back and forth at Mum and Dad; she stretched out an arm encouraging Dad to join the now uncontrollably crying group. After a while they began to quieten and separate. Nana decided to let Mum and Dad speak to the twins in private.

Turning to my Dad, she said, 'if you and Nancy need anything you know where we are,' meaning her and Grandpa. 'Bye Brent,' she said touching my Dad's cheek gently with the palm of her hand before departing.

My family flowed into the front room. I was heading down stairs now and I too went into the front room settling on the pouffe facing them as they sat together on the settee; the twins in the middle and Mum and Dad at each end. They all looked at each other unknowing who would break the silence and speak first, Mum turned her face away from them all beginning to cry again. Dad coughed trying to clear his throat, but it was Riley who spoke first.

'Josie is dead isn't she.' He spoke the words that the others couldn't at that time. Dad was the one who nodded slowly in agreement.

'Where was she Mum?' asked Minah who was now looking to Mum for clarification.

Mum patted her eyes with some tissue and said after a deep breath, 'she was found in the Hangings at the bottom of the steep hill, hidden by the overgrowth; they believed it was an accident.' Mum doubled over crying and Minah hugged her reassuringly. Mum and Dad got onto their knees in front of the twins. They were all level with each other and able now to fully appreciate an intimate hug and share their sorrow.

REALITY CHECK

If you think and say it, does it make the words more true?

I actually felt as if my heart was ripped out of my chest when Dewy disconnected, jumping from my arms and darting in to the kitchen coming to a stop under the table. I sat there feeling mentally and physically exhausted, I could have cried for all I had lost; yet still nothing.

I then realised it may not have been me holding on too tight that disturbed Dewy from our trance; I could hear movement from upstairs. Riley appeared at the top of the stairs in his blue pyjamas and slippers, and slowly started to make his way down. His eyes were red from crying and he sniffed repeatedly as one does after trying to control their sobs. He then went to the kitchen and turned the light on. I followed behind him watching him collect a cup from the draining board before going to the fridge to pour himself some milk and then sitting himself down at the kitchen table.

'You left me some?' I turned to see Minah standing in the door way, wearing her fluffy purple dressing gown and matching slippers; Riley nodded and Minah got a cup of milk before sitting herself opposite him.

'Do you think Mum and Dad have really forgiven us for killing Josie?' asked Minah looking at the cup of milk in front of her.

'What?' Riley said now looking at her. 'We didn't kill her!.'

'Had we stayed together as we were supposed to we would have seen her fall and could have gone for help,' Minah replied meeting Riley's gaze across the table.

'Maybe,' he whispered averting his gaze.

'Do you think she died hating us?' Minah asked sitting forward staring at Riley trying to get him to look at her.

I moved towards the table wanting so very much to hug them and let them know that it was not their fault.

'Me, maybe,' Riley finally said in reply. 'I did call her a dog before she left.' He began to cry. Whilst Minah left her chair to cuddle Riley and join in with his tears, she exclaimed, 'and I woofed at her!'

I remembered then, that we had argued before I left them, I had called them both brats and said aloud that I wished I had been an only child and that they deserved nothing for their ninth birthday; if only we had known then that these were our last words, we probably would have chosen better.

Dewy jumped up on to the table, for a second scaring all of us out of our wits, the twins stopped crying and as Dewy rolled onto his back assuming the position, Minah sat herself down beside Riley and they both started to rub his soft, warm belly. I now sat in the chair where Minah had been; opposite Riley, I out stretched my hand to join them in the belly rubbing. As I touched Dewy the familiar feeling of tingling came again and his vision began to over-take my own.

LEAVING

For one to truly leave everything, there must be nothing to hold them back.

I could see my past-self, coming through the front door with a large green carrier bag in my hand; I was wet from the rain outside. I took off my shoes and coat then ran upstairs.

Jumping from the table I followed my past-self swiftly up to my bedroom and made an epic leap for my bed, walked around in a circle and I then laid down.

'Dewy you rascal, you know you're not allowed in the bedrooms,' my past-self commented, whilst lying on the bed face to face with me and giving me a stroke on the head. I meowed in contentment. I watched my past-self sit at my desk and write, then swiveling around in the chair my past-self shoved a sealed envelope in front of me...

'Dewy I think they'll like the card and teddies I got them for their birthday...don't tell them!' my past-self said, putting my finger too my lips. From the bed I watched my past-self grab the green bag from the desk and shove it under the bed. 'I'll wrap them later; the card can go over here!' I watched my past-self put the card under the book on the bed side table.

'What are you two doing?' Dad's voice came from the direction of the doorway. Dewy jumped from the table and went straight out of the cat flap. My vision was my own again; opposite I could see the twins looking at each other in disbelief with a slight smile on their lips.

'What are they doing?' I heard Mum ask as she walked slowly up behind Dad to see what he was looking at. The twins got to their feet pushing the chairs out behind them, then barged past Dad and Mum, who then turned and followed them; asking each other what was going on. I watched as my family ascended the stairs, and then stopped at my bedroom door.

'What's going on?' Mum demanded to know.

'You'll see!' said Riley as Minah opened the door and turned on the light.

I made my way up after them. Standing in the door way I watched as the twins guided Mum and Dad to sit on my bed; they looked confused.

'What's going on? What's all this about?' Dad asked. Riley stepped around Minah and pulled out the card from under the book on my bed side table. Minah said

'Dewy showed us look. Look!' as Riley passed the card to Mum. Mum looked at the card then passed it to Dad; they then looked at each other before turning back to the twins.

'It's for you two,' Dad said passing it to them. I watched smiling as the twins opened the card excitedly. On the front was a picture of a teddy holding a birthday cake illuminated with candles; above the teddy's head was a banner stating *Happy Birthday To You Both*. Riley tried to read the inside aloud but couldn't get the first word out, so Minah took over.

'Riley and Minah... Proud to have a sibling like you. What's even better, I can times that by two.' She paused before reading my personal message, which I also said aloud along with her. 'I hope you both have a wonderful Birthday and realise how special and loved you are...love you more than there are stars in the night sky.... Your big Sis Josie xxx.'

Minah began to cry. Mum and Dad at some point had held hands and now pulled in the twins towards them for a loving cuddle. Meow! Dewy had come back in and made his way upstairs, stopping next to me in the door way not wanting to be told off for going into a bedroom.

'Mum!' said Riley looking at Dewy then to Mum.

'Please!' pleaded Minah. Mum looked at Dad, they both smiled.

'Come on Dewy,' they said patting the bed cover next to them. Dewy looked at me and gave one of his high pitched short purrs before springing onto my bed and receiving the fuss of his life all over his beautiful, ginger, tabby fur.

Watching my family, I knew that they would be OK.

I could feel tears welling up in my eyes and I finally began to cry whilst saying my unheard good byes and *I love you's*. As I was dissolving away into where ever I was going next, I could hear my family talking about me; and just below that I could hear a reassuring purr.

THE LAST WORD

By Georgeta Busuioc
Talent Match Specialist Mentor

Unbound is a bespoke creative writing course designed by Anita Belli. It is one of a number of projects run by the Talent Match South East project; a Big Lottery Fund project that supports 18 – 24 years old's who have been out of work for a year or more, to find relevant work or training through one-to-one mentoring support.

It illustrates how all young people, under the right guidance, can be empowered to embark on a journey which will enable them to achieve their dreams. It helps them to voice their aspirations with confidence, and values their achievements as they journey towards becoming young adults. With the guidance of tutor and writer Anita Belli, this creative writing course took its participants far beyond their original objectives.

The six young writers of Unbound, while similar in age, are a diverse group. Their backgrounds and education differ; for some, English is not their first language, while others are challenged by mental health and emotional needs. But they have demonstrated that together, with teamwork, resilience and mutual support, they can produce a book of stories and poems.

As I witnessed their progress over the course, perhaps the group's most remarkable achievement was the emerging commitment to teamwork, based on a newly-formed camaraderie of acceptance, mutual respect and support. A true sense of partnership at work. The book itself is a statement of it!

The twelve sessions of the creative writing course have also helped the participants to develop skills in areas as diverse as public speaking, presentations, problem-solving, publishing, and event organisation. It has developed their curiosity and thirst to discover their inherent creativity, which has helped them to gain confidence and enrich their self-worth. Most of all, it has helped them to emerge from their shells and discover their hidden talents.

These skills will enhance all aspects of their future, and support them in living fulfilling and independent lives.'.

ABOUT THE AUTHORS

JACK HESLOP was born and raised in Essex but can't be blamed for that. He is fond of weird fiction, poetry, history, mythology and double bacon cheese burgers. At the time of writing he is 25 years old and mildly annoyed.

AMY KITCHING born and raised in Essex, far from being a typical Essex girl, has never tanned in her life. A lover of writing, animals and music, (not always in that order). But also, grateful for the people around her and the experiences shared together.

T. KITCHING lives with her husband, children and 6 cats in the historic seaside town of Harwich. In her spare time she enjoys books, movies, walks and socialising.

TAPIWA MACHIN

Tapiwa was born and raised in Zimbabwe. She prefers to be called Tapi because some people find it hard to pronounce her full name. She is also known by other names; Shanodiwa or Shanoe. She currently lives in Essex and enjoys anything that comes her way. Tapiwa comes from a family of 4 siblings, and even though she doesn't take anything seriously, she likes nice things, which help her to achieve her goals. You can say she baits herself with the love of nice things. She's the happiest when shopping.

K. NGAI: I don't know who I am. I am nothingness. If you are reading this you are cursed! It is a lie. Who am I talking to? It is nothing – yep nothingness. My true name is .... What is it again? Ahh! It's K. I roll with it.

JOE RYAN was born in London then he moved to Essex, (yes, I know!) Spending his days locked *Inside No. 9* because in September, he will go to Hull University (yes, I know!). He likes smart blockbusters and video games.

,

C.R. MALLETT

Cherise is a small town girl, born and raised in Harwich, Essex growing up in a one parent home with 5 siblings which extended to 11 siblings to create a new family with her Step Dad. She's a happy soul, very creative, and loves to do things with her family, living a fun random life with her two wonderful children. They have Hazel by their side, a loyal Golden Labrador; Cherise also has an obsession with chicken nuggets! That is a big part of life isn't it? Cherise says: 'Although, like many of you, with a head full of dreams, thinking they won't come true; they will. You just need to believe in yourself and have a little FAITH....'

INDEX

Printed in Great Britain
by Amazon

73355337R10113